For

Rhonda

whose life is also bound with

God's golden thread of grace.

In Christ,

Pat North

OUT

OF THE

MIST

Out of the Mist is written by Patricia North
Copyright 2006, Patricia North

Published and Printed by:
  Lifevest Publishing
  4901 E. Dry Creek Rd., #170
  Centennial, CO 80122
  www.lifevestpublishing.com

Printed in the United States of America

I.S.B.N. 1-59879-103-6

OUT
OF THE
MIST

by
Patricia North

Dedication

This book is lovingly dedicated to those who live in a painful present while in wait of a joyful tomorrow.

With thanks to...

Jane Kirchoff for furnishing her
intimate journal and allowing
brief editorial additions by the author.

Shellie (North) Richards
for cover design.

My husband Dick
for preparing the manuscript.

Dr. Richard Baumgartner
for being there.

CONTENTS

"Brief quotations of scripture are taken from the Amplified Bible, Zondervan lPublishing House, Copyright 1965."

Question

I wonder;

What wonder

Lies at the core

Of this unfolding

Delicacy

Called Life?

ONE

Childhood

There was a little dip in the lawn on the north side of my house where drain pipe had once been laid. I liked to pretend it was a valley, though its depth was a mere few inches. The "valley" lent itself well to a four-year old's fantasies. One bright, snowy day I flopped on my back, made a gorgeous set of angel wings and, lying there, discovered the foreverishness of the vast sky. How big it was! How small was I! Even more staggering was the thought that someone must have made it that way.

HELLO-O-O-O-O

Are you up there, God?
Someone said You made all things.
Does that include the sky?
Here am I,
Sprawled flat against Your earth,
Wond'ring why I don't fall off;
But, even if I did,
You'd catch me, right?
I sure do hope You're there,
And not too far away,
To see these wings I've made
For Your enjoyment.

1

I had time to collect scads of luscious childhood memories; time to catch a ride on old Mr. McDonald's horse-drawn wagon a few blocks into "strange territory" without checking first with Mom, time to gather sweet peas from a vacant lot on my way home from a birthday party, time to take a weary stable horse into the woods and let him munch grass in the shade for an hour, time to carve my name in birch tree trunks for future generations to ponder, time to catch pollywogs in the creek and dangle my feet there awhile, time to slosh in puddles after a rain and squidge my toes in the warm mud, time to watch my kittens grow, time to enjoy a summer shower from the big front porch my dad built, time to climb trees all the way to the top, time to make snow-horses, time to see Roy Rogers movies twice, time to swing, time to do most anything my heart desired.

Christmas, of course, was the best time of all for gathering memories. Like any other wide-eyed child in December, I agonized through the seemingly endless month before Christmas. How time could stretch into such long days stymied me. Equally grueling were the sleepless nights when my mind churned preview after preview of how it would be on Christmas Eve.

Imagining the ecstasy of that first Christmas when Jesus was born fairly burst my being! There they were: angels, shepherds, a stable (complete with sheep, cattle, and oxen), and the Star of all stars. Nestled between Mary and Joseph was beautiful Baby Jesus. Alongside that captivating scene loomed the mystique of Santa, who would actually visit my house during the night!

I'd heard rumblings at school about the "babies" who still believed in Santa. Being a full-fledged believer I kept him to myself, secretly believing on into the fourth grade. Wanting desperately to prove my peers wrong and save Santa's reputation, I initiated a perfect plan to do both. Once school let out for vacation, I wrote to the only person with the answer.

"Dear Santa, please forget my presents this year. The only thing I want is to ride with you on your sleigh and help deliver the other children's gifts." (I figured he could save a little money on me.) Without knowing the content, Mom mailed my letter, probably wondering when her believing child would ever grow up and kick the Santa-writing ritual.

As I lay in bed that night, I imagined how beautiful it would be to float through the sky and see the world asleep while Santa delivered gifts. I hoped for a snowy, moonlit night just like Christmas cards showed.

A few days after Mom deposited my letter in the mailbox, our doorbell rang. It was the postman. For a split second I puzzled at the meaning of his words "Special Delivery for Patsy." Then my eight year old eyes caught it when Mom handed it to me. The tiny black circle said "North Pole." Without sharing my secret, I ripped open the envelope while Mom fought her curiosity and went about her work. (As soon as I had Santa's permission, I would tell all.)

The way it turned out, I had to tell Mom everything anyway. When a heart breaks, it leaks out the eyes. Mine were leaking badly. Santa said he would love to take me along, but if he did there wouldn't be room for Johnny's train or Mary's doll. Snookered. Snookered but good! Well, at least no one at school knew I had been dumb enough to believe in the old geezer. He said I could keep the enclosed good luck coin as a token of his appreciation.

I fingered the coin with one hand, and held his letter with the other as I read on. "Since Santa is so impressed with your unusual request, you may read your letter and my response in tonight's newspaper." I gasped in horror. Not only was he a fake, he was going to expose me to the whole city in that night's edition of the Port Huron Times Herald!

A few anxious hours later, I read my words and his in large, bold print - perhaps larger and bolder than any words ever printed. My full name appeared flawlessly typed in a front page article that would be read by what seemed like the whole-wide world.

My tormented mind raced ahead to the first day back to school, though Christmas hadn't yet happened; snickers of ridicule, pointing fingers, stares of unbelief. When that day came, it was every bit as awful as I had imagined.

Kids lined up on the school steps to snicker, point, and stare. Would the bell ever ring? Not before the dead of winter blew my way. Yes, it was winter in my heart; a winter of growing up and leaving precious fantasies behind – even heart beliefs. It was not only a long, long winter; it was a lonely time, when even friends doubled over with laughter at Patsy's silly idea.

It was a winter when it hurt to be me. A winter when I felt so very fragile inside. Like the icicles hanging from our eaves, breaking with just the touch of a baby finger, my emotions splintered with the tiniest word or disapproving glance. Would it ever be warm again? I doubted it with all of my broken heart.

That was the year of ice crusts. Snow fell in great mounds. Whipped by lake winds, they formed into waves, freezing into snow dunes.

3

When sleet hit the blue-white ripples, and temperatures dropped so low that cream turned into ice crystals at the top of our milk bottles, the empty lots between houses turned into one big skating rink. Occasionally, I hit a weak spot and crashed through, knee deep. That was in keeping with my emotions. It seemed like little girls fell awfully hard. By my ninth birthday, during January's deep freeze, I had become the voice of experience.

Day by miserable day, embarrassment lessened. Although my peers moved on to other more current chatter, the fact remained that I had been "had" by a myth. Spring seemed so inviting that year. Winter had dragged on forever, so when snow melted into puddles they were doubly welcomed. I just wanted to be a girl again, free of life's icy blasts. And I wanted to relive the lovely time when, as a mere child, I felt free and happy inside just to be touching my shoes to the ground.

SEVENTH SPRING

'Member how it was
In your seventh Spring?
The air had warmed
And thawed the snow
And, for the first time
Since October,
You took your boots off
And carried them.
Remember how
Fantastically light you felt –
As if your feet
Would zip right out
From under you
And maybe leave you hanging there
While they took flight?
Remember how you
Felt the cracks
In concrete sidewalks
And savored every step
Like someone in slow motion?
Remember how you
Spied the old dirt road
Near your very own house

Where your *very own mother* lived
And decided to put
The yucky boots back on
Your magic feet
Before going the rest of the way?
That was fun…
That was spring…
That was childhood,
Pressed into memory
For all time.

I was blessed with trusting parents, who thought they had been blessed with a trustworthy child. Tired of being the shy little naive kid, I attempted to forge a new image that fall. Several friends were eager to see me strut my stuff, so they gathered in a field across from my house awaiting my plan; a plan that would surely impress everyone, and smash my sissy reputation to smithereens.

While they huddled shoulder high in tall, brittle field grass, I approached my parents with a request for a couple of matches. They said "no", of course, but on my way out the back door I scooped a few wooden blue-tips from their wall container, and headed for my friends, who had formed a neat little circle within view of my house.

The parched grass caught fire on the first strike, catching us all off guard. With real fire flaring up from the field floor, I stomped fast and furious, successfully putting it out. The delight of my friends prompted me to strike a second match. Surprised that flames leaped above our heads so quickly frightened us, for no amount of foot-stomping could subdue wildfire.

With gaping jaws we hurriedly backed onto the dirt road. Within minutes the field of dried weeds was ablaze, racing toward my friend Lila's house. Where would she and her family live?

There was no real option for a mischievous girl but to fetch her dad, who could handle anything. With my frantic confession, he called the fire department, grabbed a shovel, and ran to the wildfire to chase, beat, and hose my handiwork across a city block. Waiting in my bedroom, I wondered how long the jail sentence would be for a nine-year old delinquent.

But more frightening than the thought of jail was the prospect of facing my trusting dad. I was his sweet little girl. He had never spanked me, but I was ready, willing, and almost hoping he would.

HUMILIATION

Is it so bad to disobey,
To try one's wings,
To be big
Around the little kids?
I think so –
Because,
Finally,
I looked so small
And hadn't really impressed
Anyone at all!

Childhood was like walking in and out of fog, feeling my way through a hazy maze of new experiences, learning my share of hard lessons, then emerging into bright, happy moments that made all of life seem sweet. The school scene seemed too often punctuated with harsh realities like ridicule and bullying.

Jerry was a bully. Early on I thought he threw snowballs at me because he liked me. After being clobbered on my way home for lunch a couple of days in a row, his real intentions came clear. Mom wondered why I was so late arriving home for Mrs. Grass's noodle soup, so I finally told her about Jerry.

I had sweet-talked Jerry to no avail. Pleading with him to let me pass had no effect either. All the while feeling trapped, my enormous, angry, fearful feelings were stuffed inside for self-protection. It felt more like dishonesty. Though Mom and the principal resolved the problem by calling Jerry and me in for a heart-to-heart, I left feeling badly about me. After all, I'd been two-faced with Jerry when snowballs were flying, acting nice when I felt more like choking him.

So began a pattern of seeing myself in a negative light, a pattern that would lead me into a deep, dark mist of depression further on down life's path.

My perceived cowardice was greatly reinforced the day my sixth grade classmates pummeled a shy, quiet boy during recess. Gerald was bleeding badly by the time someone ran for the teacher. As the culprits mingled among us bystanders, they issued threats to anyone considering tattling.

As soon as the frenzy settled, Mrs. Smith assembled our class, demanding to know who the guilty parties were. In a surge of conscience, I envisioned myself standing to my feet, pointing a condemning finger at the bullies, then sitting at my desk with a sense of satisfaction that justice had been done. It just didn't happen that way. Like the rest of my peers, I feared being the next victim on the way home. The air hung silent as Mrs. Smith scowled at all of us, finally giving up her search.

I suppose that was a turning point in my emotional life. Though only 10 years old (Mom started me to school at age four), I formed a negative image of myself; an image that began with the whole Santa saga, increased with Jerry's power over me, and escalated to an all-time high the day I failed to do what was right for Gerald.

I hated the feeling of giving more power to those who least deserved it. The fear factor loomed large as I lived scared, in more ways than one, from that day on. Fear was like a root that sank deep down when I compromised my integrity just for the sake of safety. And the root is what feeds the tree. There would be more occasions for feeling afraid and a failure. One of those occasions happened on a nice, warm evening.

Dad had a habit of taking Mom and me for a ride in the old '36 Chevy every evening, a habit that started when I was a squalling baby. Rides before bedtime put me to sleep. I sat in the back seat, bouncing like a rubber ball. As my head hit the seat's coarse upholstery, I sang heartily for my audience of two.

I knew every back road in the Michigan Thumb, so even when curling up half asleep, I could usually tell where we were. The size of the hill we climbed, or chuck holes that shook me awake gave unmistakable clues.

A squint of the eyes from my back seat "bed" sometimes revealed a glowing sky. That meant we were passing the oil refineries of Sarnia, Ontario – located just across the St. Clair River where our Canadian neighbors were bedding down for the night. Yellow-orange flames lit up the night sky, telling me we were heading homeward.

Foghorns from the lightship anchored at the foot of Lake Huron meant ships were plying through fog, relying on the signal to guide them safely through deep channels. Ships signaling each other far into the lake told me we were taking the lake shore route. A kid can learn a lot from the back seat of a beat-up car, out for a ride at dusk.

I learned more than I wanted to know about life the night we returned home from a lakeshore ride. Suddenly coming into view of our headlights was a team of runaway horses. Their frenzied gallop swerved the wagon behind them on and off the road. Traffic coming from the other direction was unaware of the danger, so Dad immediately cooked up a plan.

He told Mom to get in the driver's seat so he could jump off the running board onto the wagon and rein in the horses. She and I were hysterical at the thought. Her resistance to try such a thing, and my crying, created a delay that proved deadly, though it's obvious such a plan would have been undoable anyway.

In just a matter of minutes the horses crossed center and collided with an oncoming car, resulting in a huge fireball that lit up the evening sky. Dad was put out with Mom and me for interfering with his effort to change the situation. Without knowing the people involved, he grieved for whoever had met up with the team of runaways. He took us to a nearby tavern to call police, then drove us home, anguished that such a beautiful evening could produce such enormous tragedy.

When Dad went to work the next day, he learned that the man who was killed in the fiery collision had been his co-worker. As he lamented the fact that his unexecuted plan could have saved the man's life, I assumed a degree of guilt for keeping him from it. He could have been a hero if it hadn't been for me.

Without realizing it, life's little lessons about loss, remorse, vulnerability, anger, and all the in-betweens were piling up. None of it was pretty; none of it - Jerry, bullies, or death.

LIFE

I think that boys are very mean,
And life's too big, from what I've seen.
Foolish boys, they hurt each other.
I'm so afraid
Away from Mother.
People go for rides and die,
And I,
I wonder 'bout the big, sad sky.

Though peppered with sad and scary times, those early years were also salted with yummy events, such as our annual treks to the mushroom patch - *our* mushroom patch!

Every fall, when the air began to chill a bit, and rain pelted the earth, we stuffed sacks and pails into the trunk of our black Chevy and drove north to an old gravel road that held the best harvest of Shaggy Manes around. After a long day at school, catching sight of the car with a dented right fender parked at the intersection, meant we were going straight to the mushroom patch. Sometimes our mounting excitement burst like a bubble, when intruders had beaten us to the punch, or there weren't enough shaggies to fill a fist. Still, we returned frequently to pluck so many tall, white treasures that we could hardly bag them all.

All the way home I salivated and dreamed of what was to come that evening. After all of us rubbed the shaggy part off the mushrooms with our thumbs, then rinsed them well, they were tossed into a bowl to bob around until Mom performed her culinary magic. Times were tough for my parents. Free food, whether mushrooms or speared fish, dipped herring or smelt, was a welcomed gift. But mushrooms, ala Mom, made the best feast.

First, Mom got out the iron skillet and put a generous dollop of "butter" in it. Butter in our home consisted of the white lard-like block of stuff that took on a yellow butter appearance, but only after hands had kneaded it thoroughly with a dark, orange-red tablet of some sort. Regardless, my taste buds couldn't tell the difference. When the fat sizzled, Mom dropped lots of chopped, clean mushrooms into the skillet, salted and peppered them, and stepped back for a brief, mouth-watering wait.

Bread, slathered with "butter", lay as yawning jaws on plates. Mom, spoon in hand, scooped our steaming treasure on each slice, making the most luscious treat of fall. More salt and pepper, more hot mushroom sandwiches, and all was well with my world.

A bonus I enjoyed while at the mushroom patch was the sight and sound of a little creek nearby. It swelled during mushroom season, so I often studied the ways of water while picking mushrooms. Water – always moving. Always interesting. Always singing a melody to anyone who'd listen, no matter how meager the trickle. Somewhere deep inside I wanted to be like a waterway, not realizing then that waterways create fog - mist that hides the beauty and causes disorientation for travelers who've never passed that way before. Life would offer challenges for me when the mist rolled in. Meanwhile, I clung to the memories my mother made for me.

MOM

My Mom is best
At building memories;
The kind that bulge
With warmth and happiness,
And lessons worth the learning.
She'd take an ordinary day,
Or circumstance,
And decorate it
With her special touch –
That touch will be
A part of me
When I get old and gray!

As I watched my Tom Mix spurs glow in the dark one night, I thought how frightening it would be to grow up and leave home. In spite of the monsters and lions that prowled through my room, and under my bed nightly, home seemed to be the best thing going.

My only sibling, Jack, left home to sail the Great Lakes when I was seven. Even though he wearied of having me underfoot (especially when his girlfriend blinked her big, brown eyes in his direction), he missed me enough to write Pig-Latin letters quite often. His mundane task of "watching Patsy" was a thing of the past, and his time at home had ended. From then on, I lived as an only child.

While Jack sailed the S.S. Penobscot, I rode the range on sawhorses Dad made for his tomboy girl. Holding tightly to reins of rope, I imagined my side yard was vast western desert land and my sidekicks, Edith and Margaret, were Roy and Dale. Our trail rides ended with Mom's call to lunch and a sideway leap off our pillow saddles.

Dad wasn't much fun, being a rather depressed, negative, angry person; but one winter day he made a memory worth the keeping. A heavy snowfall blanketed the ground during the night, so he commenced clearing the long sidewalk, shovel in hand. I don't recall who threw the first snowball, but we had a battle royal.

Dad ducked and laughed as I whacked him with a couple of good shots. Making Dad laugh felt like I had accomplished something huge. I let him pelt me, too. The hilarity ended all too soon, but not before Mom captured the moment on film…black and white, of course.

One other humorous incident with Dad happened the night Mom somehow convinced him to dress up for a Halloween masquerade party. He went as a clown. Neighbors took charge of me for the evening, and when Dad and Mom returned for me they were in stitches. Dad nearly doubled over laughing as he described the scene at the door of the party place.

His clown costume was a one-piecer, and the tickets were in his back pants pocket, underneath his outfit. Unable to get into the party without his tickets, he had to go through all kinds of contortions to reach them through his costume's back seam. Clowns remind me of Dad's happy night.

Most people didn't understand why Dad was such a somber sort, but I did. That's why it was no surprise to me that he took so quickly to a stray dog that wandered into his garage with bleeding paws one night. Hughie to the rescue! The pooch flopped down on a pile of rags Dad used for his part-time auto repairs, revealing worn down paw pads. Dad said the mutt had probably been left behind when its former owners moved, and wore out its feet following their scent.

Dad patted and comforted the dog with soft conversation, sending me inside for warm milk and food. Mom obliged within minutes. The three of us watched intently as the exhausted pooch lapped milk from Dad's cupped hand, being too weak to lift its head. There was that unmistakable, unfailing compassion on Dad's countenance again. It appeared at the most unexpected times, usually when someone or something needed rescuing. It might have been a mystery to most people how Dad could be so caustic at times, yet so tender in moments like those. But I knew…

When Dad was four his father was burned while making repairs inside a boiler. Someone unwittingly turned on the power too soon, causing severe burns to the grandfather I never met. After two years of hospitalization, he died. To pay mounting medical bills, Dad's mother found employment and placed her three children in a boarding home -orphanage institution in London, Ontario. She returned each Friday to visit and pay for their care. One ordinary Friday the family's world turned inside out and upside down.

Authorities took matters into their own hands, placing the children out for adoption. The baby died in a fall from the high chair at the boarding home, doubling the woman's grief and leaving Dad and his sister, Pearl. Pearl was 6. When Dad's mother was informed of the adoptions, she collapsed.

The scene at the boarding home earlier that day could well have been taken from a Hollywood horror film. The children were standing together in the front doorway when a car drove up and parked at the curb, as if waiting for someone. The someone was Pearl. She had been adopted by a sweet, older widow lady who longed for companionship. She felt that a little girl would fill the bill.

As Pearl was led down the sidewalk, away from Hughie toward the waiting car, she reached out for him. He reached out for her, and as the two of them realized they were being separated, their shrieks pierced the surrounding area. They tried in vain to change the course of events, but within minutes their screams faded into sobs.

Pearl soaked her pillow with tears of sorrow all weekend. Hughie did the same. Seeing how inconsolable Pearl was about leaving her little brother behind, the lady decided to return for him Monday morning. She guessed she could manage two as easily as one if they loved each other THAT much. Pearl stopped her crying and perked up as if going to a birthday party when she heard the wonderful news. But Monday morning didn't prove to be party time. It was perhaps the second saddest day of her young life.

About an hour before Pearl and her new "mother" arrived to get Hughie, he was taken by another family. They were already on their way to Sarnia, Ontario where the family owned a dry cleaning - laundry business. Hughie's new family consisted of two alcoholic parents and their disgruntled daughter, Margaret. Margaret didn't like the competition of a four year old boy, and made it her mission to make life miserable for him from day one. Her parents did more than their share to assist.

The mistreatment Dad received as daily fare resulted in somber, reactive, non-trusting behavior that became a permanent part of him. Was it any wonder that Dad took so well to a beleaguered dog flopped flat on a pile of rags? Dad had been there.

For several days, the dog got VIP treatment. As his paws healed, and he gained strength, his tail wagged vigorously in gratitude. I thought homely old George, Dad's hunting hound, might have a new coop-mate. Then one frosty morning the inevitable happened. We awoke to find our visitor gone. He had slipped out through the "bad weather hole" Dad had cut in the wall for George. Dad said the dog would probably keep going until he found his family.

I detected a note of longing in his voice. It didn't seem fair that a dog could find its family when Dad had been without one for decades – until Pearl's relentless search discovered his whereabouts

From the time Pearl was a little girl, leaving the orphanage without her brother a second time, she determined to find him. When she finally got old enough, she made connection with someone who obtained Dad's records. She learned that he had been moved to Port Huron, Michigan, just across the river from Sarnia. To Dad's amazement, Pearl made contact with him. He had reached the mid-teens by then, still a minor. His family put a stop to communications, confiscating all of Pearl's letters. At least, they thought so. Secret meetings and letters sent elsewhere kept the two siblings in touch.

Meanwhile, Dad endured continued abuse. During one of his mother's drunken stupors she knocked him to the floor, stood on his spine, and stayed there until he cried. As he lay there he decided that she would never make him cry again. Oh, Hughie would cry again. Much later! But she wouldn't be the one to make him cry.

Dad came to hate his dismal existence - until he met Marguerite at work when her machine broke down. His quick response to the crisis, with expert mechanical skills, set the scene for many convenient machinery breakdowns. Marguerite was all of 15. Hugh was 21.

Their brief romance flamed into a quick marriage. Mom was a week shy of being 16 when Dad walked out of his home for the last time. It was the dead of January. With no coat of his own, he had sister Margaret's heavy sweater on. She made him take it off before walking to his bride-to-be parents' house for the wedding.

Bitter winter temperature couldn't chill the joy he felt upon leaving that family, which turned out not to be his adoptive family at all. They had just been foster parents all those years. That was discovered when he became a naturalized American citizen in the early 1940s. Rather than change his name (he had two children by then), he left it as was.

Once Dad married, he and Aunt Pearl had many reunions. Each summer our little family went through border customs to enter Dad's homeland, Canada. Crossing the huge Blue Water Bridge was an exhilarating experience for a little girl. Aqua-marine waters of St. Clair River stretched out on one side, and the vibrant blue waters of Lake Huron went as far as eye could see on the north side. Bright, white Fort Gratiot lighthouse stood on the shoreline of Lake Huron, right near the mouth of the river, resembling a stalwart sentinel guarding the waterways. Sailboats dotted the glistening lake, their full-blown canvases catching lake breezes like big butterfly nets.

Sometimes, a glance downward revealed the deck of a massive lake freighter passing under the bridge as we headed for one of my

13

favorite spots - Aunt Pearl's unique and stately country home. There, while sipping iced tea and eating her tough pie crust, I would once more hear the tale of her and Dad's separation and reunion.

Pearl's house was a two-story red brick that had perched at the top of a sloping corner lot for 150 years. The lot was surrounded by farm fields and lined with tall, gracefully drooping evergreen trees. In spite of no running water, her house was immaculate. Bold, splashy wallpaper hugged the walls, and a fireplace adorned every room, upstairs and down.

Even without the luxury of air conditioning, the old house stayed cool inside; nice and comfy for storytelling. It has since gone the way of modern civilization. Sad to say, "progress" put a gas station in its place. Before being erased from the lovely landscape, however, the chicken coop-turned-playhouse and fascinating tales of my heritage made their way into my already teeming memory bank.

My high school years held two beautiful surprises. Both had an enduring impact. Just a few weeks short of my 15th birthday, Prince Charming charged from out of the foggy teens, into my heart. It might be more accurate to say he just appeared, thanks to my cousin, Janice. Jan notified me that a new minister had arrived at the church I had attended in earlier years, complete with two daughters and three sons.

One of those sons was a very boyish looking 16 year old named Dick. She thought it might be worth my time to take a look-see. I had seen Dick six months earlier, actually, when he played the piano for my grandfather's funeral. As suggested by Janice, I went to church to take a more serious look.

I wore a navy-blue turtle neck sweater and checkered skirt the first time I went through church doors to give the preacher's family a once-over. Being the timid girl I was, I sat in back and simply observed. I wasn't quite ready for romance, but romance galloped in before I had tasted my 15th birthday cake. That was just 16 days after our eyes met.

Mom and Dad went for a ride without me one Sunday afternoon, shortly after I had met Dick at a youth meeting. While they were gone, the phone rang. It was Dick, inviting me to go for a ride that afternoon with another couple. For some curious reason I abandoned my shyness and said "yes." My parents arrived in time to chuckle, along with me, at the thought that someday – bye and bye – I could tell my children that I had once upon a time dated a preacher's son.

The boyish looking guy had my attention from the start. He was everything I had outlined in my mind for the kind of fellow I'd hold out for - kind, polite, responsible, sensitive, motivated, stable, and spiritual.

He was everything the mean schoolboys I had known were not. Being only 14, I was hardly used to dates, so I fluttered with nervous anticipation as I awaited the arrival of Dick and the other twosome.

Dick and I sat stiffly apart, though he took the liberty of putting his arm around my shoulders. That's just the way boys were back then. A ride in the car meant an arm wrapped around the girl's shoulders. This girl didn't like that move, but I did like Dick. By the end of another date or two I had set my heart, like flint, toward him. And he set his heart, like flint, toward the girl in the navy blue sweater. I had turned 15, he had turned 17 when our journey began.

Like most "going steady" kids, we passed our share of notes in high school corridors, but when Dick went off to college a year after we met, notes changed into letters. Two and a half years of our courtship were spent via the U.S. Mail. Those were lonely years, but I had no doubt about the rightness of "us." I watched the mailbox like a mother hen watches her chicks.

After disembarking the school bus each weekday, I scooped up the precious letter from Illinois, with its upside-down stamp and SWAK letters scrawled on the flap, and hurried into the house. After throwing my pile of books down, I sank in my rocker to devour Dick's captivating words, like luscious lollipops. A day without a letter was like a candle without a flame.

For the first time since he'd left for college, several days went by without hearing from him. Maybe it's exam time, I thought. I knew he was the one for me, so I was confident (almost) that all was well. He was likely just busy. Yet, some little twinge of uneasiness lingered. Just to chide him, I wrote big, bold letters across the back of a postcard, "Why?" My girlfriend, Lila - whose house I had nearly demolished in the grass fire years before - laughed with me as I dropped the card in the mailbox downtown. Maybe THAT would get a rise out of him!

An hour or so later, I arrived home from school to find a letter from Dick. Oh, if only I hadn't sent the postcard. Well, he could take a joke. But the joke was on me, and it didn't leave me laughing.

Racing into the house, I dropped my books on the couch, and sank once more into the rocker to gobble up his long-overdue words. Hm-m-m! He forgot the SWAK. He must be VERY busy to have left out such an important ingredient.

Dick said he didn't want to hurt me, but he had met a girl. I swallowed hard. We were history. Several hours later, I was still sitting in the chair, letter in hand, staring at the cold, linoleum floor. Someone turned on a light. I couldn't move. Not much was said. Moms and dads have a way of knowing when to let life happen, hurt and all.

The night two horses crossed center and exploded into a blazing inferno had no more impact than the letter I held in my hand. But I grew up a bit during those agonizing hours, and made some decisions. I would not write first. I would not chase him, even though I knew that he and I were special. I would wait for him to make the same discovery, and I would feel my way through present fog into an unknown future.

A month or so later, Dick came home for a weekend service in which he and members of his college quartet would sing. I received a call as soon as he got in town asking if he could see me. I said it would be okay, determined not to do the falling. He would have to do that. I felt he would. Before the evening ended, he asked me to be his girl again. It was easy. I had never really stopped.

Dick told me how awful he felt when he received my "Why?" card. He thought it had been written in response to his letter. I was secretly glad they had crossed in the mail.

My high school graduation was fast approaching in the spring of '54. Just after I had gone to bed one night, the second remarkable event of my young life plopped me in my rocker once again. Dad had just turned in, too, so Mom answered the phone. I heard her note of alarm when she called Dad to the phone.

"Hugh, it's Pearl!" We didn't get late night calls, and calls from Pearl were rare, so I jumped out of bed and leaned on the doorjamb. Dad lumbered out of his bedroom, wondering what calamity had hit Pearl's family, knowing that long distance calls most often meant trouble in those days.

Within a few short minutes, Dad placed the phone in its cradle, and sank onto the couch. Tears glistened as he reported an unbelievable thing: "Pearl has found our mother!"

Dad was 48 when he got his mother back. I was 17 when my grandmother entered my life. It was enough to take our breath away; but we actually gulped in a lot of air as Dad spun off details.

Pearl had made a lifelong habit of reading the obituary column each night in hope of one day seeing a name that might have connection to her biological family. Being older than Dad, she remembered more about her family. That night she read along as usual…until a name leaped off the page, straight into her remembrance. The name of a deceased person's survivor was listed as Alice Head Allen. Alice Head. That was her mother's maiden name!

16

Pearl immediately tracked down the phone number of the Allen family to inquire about Alice Head. She said, "I'm Pearl." There was no hesitation at the other end of the line: "Oh, yes, Mother has told us about you and Hughie!"

My grandmother had suffered several small strokes in recent days, so the advisability of startling her with such profound news was carefully discussed. It was quickly decided that her prolonged grieving over the loss of her first family should come to an end. The family tried to plan a safe strategy for breaking the incredible news, but there was no gentle way. She was simply told that her beloved Pearl and Hughie had been found. Shock gave way to sheer joy as the short, white-haired lady with twinkly eyes and a smile as wide as the past 44 years of separation, joined in plans for a grand two-family reunion within the month.

Memorial Day weekend 1954, Mom, Dad and I went through customs with an edge of anxiety, hoping the officers would let us pass with no delay. A quick glance under the seats (to be sure we weren't sneaking any goods across the border) and we were on our merry way.

It was a glorious, sunshiny day. The lake panorama of sailboats and lake freighters on sky-blue water seemed especially vivid. By the time we would return that evening, the stately white lighthouse would welcome home a completed family. What a perfect day to get a grand-mother!

Since Pearl had already met Grandma and her family, we went straight to her home so she could take us to the reunion site, which was my half-uncle's house. She chattered all the way, adding to the excite-ment we already felt. When we arrived, the entire family rushed outside to greet us. Grandma hugged Dad as if she'd never let go, and Dad smiled more that day than he had probably smiled his whole lifetime.

Once again, a day was spent listening to stories from the past. Grandma talked about the heartaches she'd endured after her husband's industrial accident. She clung tightly to Dad as she relived her efforts to work and be sure her children were cared for, as well as her anguish upon being told that they had been placed elsewhere...permanently.

That was Canada in the early 1900s. Could things have been so cruelly managed then, or was Grandma hiding her guilt for leaving them? Could children really have been removed from their family without parental knowledge or consent? Watching Grandma cling to Dad and Pearl, it just didn't matter. It was clear beyond a doubt how deeply she loved her Hughie – my emotionally wounded dad. Those wounds remained until the last day of his 92 years, leading to alienation from nearly every family member, including me. His mother was the exception.

My brand new, perky, toothless grandmother waved good-bye until we drove out of sight. Dad and Mom talked all the way home, but I pondered the amazing turn of events in my 17 year old life. Dad had found his family, but I had gained a whole new family, too!

As usual, we motored up the hump of lofty Blue Water Bridge, scanning the sparkling blue deeps of the two-toned waterway. Predictably, Fort Gratiot lighthouse towered above treetops like a pretty white guard, stuck in a base of sand. I hoped the bridge wouldn't cave in with us still on it, then breathed a sigh of relief once above land. I could see the church where I'd met the love of my life just a block away as we descended. We were home.

I was about to graduate from high school. Exactly one year later, I would marry my future preacher-to-be husband in the church we had just passed. Following our simple but nice wedding, we would leave houses and lands and peoples for a life of ministry. I was all for that, but I didn't realize the enormous emotional load that I would drag along with me - not just Dad's load, but mine, too.

My teen years were a bit different than those of my peers. I was a loner, except for Dick and a few friends at church. With Dad's moodiness and frequent angry spells, it was too risky to have girls visit or stay overnight. When he was happy, he was *really* happy – almost giddy. When he was angry, I walked on eggs.

Regardless of his moods, he faithfully drove me to church. Eventually, he and Mom joined the church, but his negative, touchy disposition made healthy relationships impossible. He gave up on Christians, but held onto a certain thread of faith in God that enabled him to respect the course I'd chosen.

Adults in the church knew Dad's volatile temper and sharp tongue. They also knew I returned to church to find a boyfriend: their preacher's son. So, word trickled back to me from time to time that a few folks thought Dick could have done better. I felt inferior, even in Dick's family, but our relationship escalated to the marriage altar anyway. I was 18 when I left home for a new life – a life that would soon take a turn for the worse.

The load I dragged into marriage was a sense of being second class. I fretted about every little thing, much as Dad did. My psychic skin seemed particularly thin, leaving me with lots of hurt feelings from comments that likely weren't meant to hurt. I was so unsure of myself that

18

conversation didn't come easily. I felt conspicuous in public, and dreaded even getting on a bus.

Somewhere along the road of childhood, I withdrew from life's natural course to good emotional health. It wasn't until the unexpected stresses of marriage presented themselves that I experienced profound fear of the future. Insecurity sank a deep root and, as I had learned when a child, the root is what feeds the tree.

Dick and I moved four times our first four months of marriage. A month here, a month there, then out of state so he could resume college studies. We ended up in a tiny 8 by 25 foot trailer on campus. With no car, we hoofed it or took a bus to town. My groom worked nights and attended classes days, leaving his new bride alone.

All the monsters that invaded my bedroom as a little girl appeared during my adult nights. I cried and moaned as I searched the skies outside my itty bitty bedroom window, wondering how to be better. Brooding about my moods, they got even darker. I frightened myself with the thought that something must be wrong with me. Somewhere in the shadows of unshared fears, I became convinced that I was unsatisfactory.

TWO

So This Is Life!

When we married, I was not only scared of my shadow, I was scared of the whole, wide, adult world. I half-heartedly agreed to help finance the rest of Dick's education, but the expectation angered me. My four months of employment before the wedding proved nigh unto impossible, though the job came easily. I was among the fastest responders at the telephone company call board, but being around people was terrifying.

It was a different world out there, not the protective, secluded home I had known, where nothing was expected of me but to be a good kid. The people around me seemed so confident and world-wise. Why wasn't I?

The bus trip to work was a dread, as were working hours. I was almost too timid to pull the "get-off" cord. Walking past the fire station, where men sat gawking and talking, was cause for taking the long way around. Being late for work didn't matter. Avoiding their stares was worth the risk.

Working with strangers felt like facing mountain upon mountain. My days off were spent crying, dreading the thought of going back to work. I hurt far too much over ordinary things. Brooding about why I was so odd became daily fare.

Brooding quickly turned into full-blown depression, and depression mushroomed into morbidity. Though only 18, I thought a lot about suicide, taking excess aspirin to see if they'd make me sleep...or forget. Without words, I was telling Dick that his new wife couldn't handle life. We were young; too embarrassed and confused to share the strange events with anyone.

Dick had numerous school responsibilities, as well as a full time job. He was editor of the college newspaper for a small stipend, held a class office, worked nights, carried a full class load, and tried desperately to help his floundering wife adapt to a new lifestyle.

After three months of agony, I quit my job. Our first baby was on the way. So was a rocky financial road. Amidst anticipation of a baby-to-be, we struggled with the fact that I was not up to the simplest of life's demands. We hid it well. Therefore, no help came.

Driving along a city street late one night, our headlights flashed on cemetery tombstones. I shuddered, envisioning my name on every one of them. Regardless, the grim sight of tombstones began to hold an eerie, beckoning power. Day and night they loomed large before me. A satin comforter, one of our wedding gifts, became a death shroud. I imagined it lining my own casket. What in the world was wrong with me?

We were sinking in every way. There was not enough money, of course, to pay our bills. Dick's grades were slipping. It didn't make sense for me to be home with no responsibilities, no activities, no family (yet), no visible sickness; just a terror of being in the world. Who would understand? Maybe my childhood playmates were right – I was just plain spoiled. They said so when I got lots of Christmas presents one year. I suspected their parents had said that about me around the dinner table, and that hurt.

Now I wondered what people said about me as I walked down the street. The seed planted so long ago had taken root – and "the root is what feeds the tree." That root flourished in a too-sensitive heart. I was in big trouble.

One lonely night, as I sat in silence, two mice crawled out of the closet. They had come up through a crack in the flooring. I shivered at the sight of them, so they scurried away. As each night came and went, they reappeared. I was alarmed to find myself expecting them. Before long I had no reaction. Matter-of-factly, I decided I was going crazy. Dick was at work when I came to that conclusion.

School finally dismissed, and we went back to stay with my parents for the summer. Dick found a temporary job in another town, which lasted until his return to college. The baby was due in a week; so I stayed behind, promising to call him the minute labor began. We had a car by then, thankfully.

The next Friday afternoon, Dick came home in time to take me to the hospital for the delivery of eight pound Steven Randall. He was beautiful beyond our expectations, what with his pearly skin, bright, rosy

21

cheeks, and shock of dark hair. We were proud to have such a healthy, handsome son. A severe infection kept me and the baby from going home with Dick, but three weeks later our little family returned to Illinois. Barely recovered from my miserable infection, I began the treacherous job of parenting.

While Dick spent late afternoons and evenings at work, I tended our newborn. His bassinet was crammed between the only three pieces of furniture we owned. On the tiny kitchen counter perched a portable miniature five-gallon wringer washer kettle. The contraption allowed me to wash a few diapers at a time, but when we had saved enough quarters to go to the campus laundromat, I packed up laundry, detergent, and baby for a walk down the gravel road.

The wash house was a cold, lonely place. I liked the aloneness, though. That way no one could detect my lack of expertise in baby care and laundry procedures. Steve lay on the folding table as I dropped hard-to-come-by coins into machines that sloshed and whirled our laundry. After lugging baskets, boxes, and baby home, I turned on the radio to hear Arthur Godfrey croon about Hawaii, then waited for the mice. No matter how many traps we set, they managed to re-populate.

The four months following Steve's birth, our lives spiraled downward. Depressions were more frequent and severe. Dick experienced a great sense of failure in school, knowing his parents had high hopes for him becoming a pastor, and excelling in his class. We felt like we had let the whole world down, even though so few in the world were aware we existed.

One January morning we packed the car we couldn't pay for with Steve and a few worldly belongings and headed back to Michigan. Before leaving campus, we stopped at the school post office for a last batch of mail when Dick's brother –also a student – passed by. We didn't mention leaving. Heavy, guilty hearts weighed us down as we drove away from campus for the last time. That load of guilt stuck with us for a decade.

The three of us bounced around from household to household for several weeks, until Dick landed a job in the machine-tool industry in Detroit. It was during that traumatic transition that we discovered our second child was on the way. We were renting the upstairs of my aunt and uncle's home when I broke the news to Aunt Winnie. She tried to temper her surprise and disapproval, but the message was clear. I had once again fallen short of people's pleasure in me. The feeling of embarrassment took root that day; and the root is what feeds the tree. I began resenting the new baby before he was even born.

Many months later Jimmy arrived. Steve was only 14 months old. I was deeply troubled during my 5 days of hospital confinement. Feeling that no one approved of our growing family, I dove into a deep postpartum depression, not bonding with the baby at all, but withdrawing. The nurse scolded me for not adequately feeding him. He cried between feedings, making it necessary for the staff to fill him up. I couldn't muster up enough concern or energy to help out.

When they brought him in every four hours, I put the bottle in his mouth and left it up to a newborn to decide. If he drank, fine. If he didn't, they were well paid for taking care of him. No one seemed to notice that I was a new mother with major depression. I didn't verbalize my dark feelings or fears, so I went home with two babies to tend, emotionally unequipped to properly mother either of them.

In following months, my lows got lower. Fearful that someone might see me crossing the street to get the mail, I left it there for Dick to pick up after work. The babies were too much. I felt hopeless and overwhelmed with the dawning of each new day. With no reserve to draw from, and knowing the problem wasn't going to go away by itself, I made my first good adult decision; a decision arising out of a mother's innate love for her children. I asked my doctor for help.

I was referred to a psychologist who set up a meeting with my husband and me the week after Christmas. Waiting in the office, I leafed through dog-eared magazines wondering how I had ended up in a shrink's office.

The doc wasn't what I expected, which was a fatherly, compassionate type. Rather, he bluntly asked if I thought I was losing my mind. With a few tears, I admitted I did. He said, "Well, don't flatter yourself. You have an anxiety neurosis. It you agree to be hospitalized, you can be well in one month." - the amount of time insurance would cover. We were desperate. It sounded worth a try. After all, there were eighteen years of parenting ahead, and I had scarcely scraped through sixteen months.

We went home to make arrangements for the care of our little boys, bought some slippers for the hospital stay, and prepared for my admission to the psychiatric unit of a small Detroit hospital.

January 4th I got some new room mates. The unit nurse was very kind. It didn't seem like such a bad place. In fact, there was an air of levity that surprised me, and a noticeable bond of affection between patients. I settled in for the "cure."

Electro-shock therapy was administered three times a week. The M.D. reminded me of a zany little man in some goofy movie flick. His greeting to one and all was predictable. With a fake French accent, he tossed each of us a cheery "Good day, madame!" Then, with a flick of his wrist, he injected a sedative and disappeared from view as his words bounced away on receding waves of consciousness.

The cold metal conductors placed on my temples sent umpteen volts of electricity through my brain as the "kind" nurse looked on. Hours later I awoke, wondering how the cure was progressing. The only difference I noticed was a loss of memory.

The psychologist who arranged for my treatment made frequent visits to the hospital. We invariably sat in chairs lined against the busy hallway wall. "How are you doing?" he asked. "Fine."

"Great. That's just great!" he always replied. I was too young and naive to know that was therapy time. At age 20, I just thought he was being nice. These conversations were to the tune of $30 per visit; big money in the 50s. I learned about the cost later.

One Sunday afternoon my parents brought the babies for a visit. After they left my situation closed in on me. I felt trapped, like the time Jerry wouldn't let me go home. I didn't especially want to go home. And I wasn't ready to care for the boys. But I wanted to know I could leave. So I asked. Sensing their alarm, I reminded staff that when I was admitted voluntarily I was told I could leave the same way.

They tried pacifying me, which increased my agitation. I told my husband to take me home. He looked bewildered, caught between a rock and a hard place. The nurse got on the phone with my psychologist and explained the situation. He, in turn, spoke with Dick and instructed him to transport me to a nearby mental health facility. Unable to hear the instructions, I ran out to the car in my robe and new slippers to wait for him. Upon hearing the doctor's words, Dick decided the man didn't know any more about my problems than he did, and took me home.

A few days cool-off helped me realize my still-present need. I agreed to re-enter the hospital. The second reception was not as cordial as the first. A brusque nurse met me, led me to a tiny cubicle which housed some surgical patients, and told me to "stay put." I was scared. Now that they had me back, and my husband was gone, what would they do with me? The crisp nurse had obviously been told about my quick exit.

As I stared at the walls of my "cell," I regretted my decision to return. Bracing myself for the consequences of earlier behavior, I swal lowed hard and fought rising tears. There was no place to run; no way to reach Dick.

I ventured to the doorway of the dingy, windowless room just in time to spot an angel coming down the hallway. The friendly nurse who had first welcomed me to the hospital swept into my room with a yard-wide smile, latched her arm around mine, and led me back to my room-mates. I felt released from prison as we left that wing of the hospital and walked to more familiar territory where a slightly stale birthday cake awaited. I had turned twenty-one. Would this be the year I would get out of my emotional prison?

Because of my "good progress", treatment ended after 3 weeks. The psychologist often called the house to see how things were. "How're you doing? Great! That's just great. May I talk with your husband?" It was nice of him to be checking things out with Dick, I thought. Much later I learned why he called so regularly; he wanted his money for "pro-fessional services rendered." Since the quality of professional services I'd received from him were so lacking, it was a long, long time before I trusted anyone in his profession again.

Back to the drudgery of changing diapers, washing bottles, lis-tening to crying babies, and being alone with them 11 hours a day. Down I went. Shock therapy hadn't helped. I was more depressed than ever. One bright, sunny day I sat at the table, stared out the window, and summed it all up in these words:

Life is like a dark and gloomy corridor
Where sunlight never filters in…

Sunshine seemed to be ever on the outside. How to get it within was beyond me. Though I couldn't reach out, a few people managed to reach into the dark places of my life and help me. I was scheduled for several outpatient shock therapies at the county mental health hospital, which had a bad reputation. It was the same place my husband had refused to take me the day I panicked.

Dick had missed a lot of work. With the doctor pressing for his many "counseling" fees, our pastor and his wife offered to take me for treatment as often as needed. Those gentle folks had pastored the church of my childhood. Now they were shepherds of a different sort; taking me safely through the busy streets of Detroit to spend several hours of their day waiting for me to wake up. They never pressed for conversation or gave advice. They were simply there.

A burly young orderly, who resembled the Hollywood stereotype of mean attendants, escorted me to the treatment area. His massive appearance suggested trouble for any uncooperative patient. My heart thumped uncontrollably as I meekly followed him to the padded table. When he finally spoke, however, my fears died. His physical hulk just matched a warm, compassionate nature. The gentleman was one of those pleasant surprises that makes the going easier behind real and imaginary iron gates.

Months slipped by without the benefit of much of my memory. It had been shocked to near oblivion. But the real problem hadn't been touched. Still, change was appealing. On our older son's second birthday, we moved into a new home and town. It had been eight months since the hospitalization. A new house looked very inviting. I busied myself with decorating and settling in. Maybe the fog would lift with new surroundings and a new start.

Dick continued to work long hours, with added travel time. Twelve hours a day, six days a week, he was gone. Sundays were consumed with church activities. (He directed the choir for extra income.) While I sneaked in an afternoon snooze, Dick often did the dishes and played with the boys.

I kept to myself the first year. It was too hard to be social with two little tykes wanting to go outside. The next summer I found myself more out than in. Talking didn't come easily, so I did some good listening. A couple of neighbors befriended me, breaking some of the loneliness. One of them took me to get my driver's license when Jimmy was a toddler. That gave me a bit of freedom, if I wanted to pay the price of wakening kiddies and driving Dick to work in Detroit.

Jimmy always had car sickness early on, but when the walls closed in too much we took daddy to work and got out in the big, bustling world for awhile. A baby step in the sight of others was a giant step to me.

Moving had its advantages, but my inner monsters moved with me. Unconquered monsters are like that. During the eight years we lived in that house, nightmares manifested in screams that traveled throughout the neighborhood. Dick often rushed in from his late night studies to find me jolted upright in bed. After assuring me everything was alright, he returned to his books and I returned to my nightmares.

There were two persistent nightly terrors. The first was a tall man who entered my bedroom and either stood staring at me, or moved toward me. Sometimes he chased me. The figure was an enemy, whose presence tormented me.

The second nightmare was that of twisting, writhing, coiled, ugly snakes - ugly beyond description. The horrid dreams seemed to have no end. With a throat that ached from turning inside out the night before, I sometimes looked in the mirror and said, "You're crazy." The hopeless eyes staring back at me were mine – full of fear and pain. I couldn't find my way out of the confusing fog.

Unsuccessful attempts to relate to relatives and neighbors occasionally got me embroiled in this or that controversy. My inability to rationally or confidently discuss the smallest of issues led to a total loss of control. Then Dick would pick up the pieces, running interference with those involved, and make it all better. I let him do that. But as it happened more and more frequently, I felt less able to manage my own life.

I was a little girl in an adult body, expecting him to cover my messy tracks, rescue me from myself, and be what I wasn't. He did a good job of it. His patience was limitless. It should have come as no surprise that he soon developed his own peculiar set of symptoms. One spring day, we awoke to double trouble.

THREE

Locked In, Wanting Out

Dick had given up a great dream for us, his family. By 1959 we had a daughter Shellie and our two sons to consider. The shame of slinking away from college was taking a toll on him. Worse yet, running from the call of God was eating him alive. Dissatisfied at work, he began to brood about not fulfilling his goal of being a pastor. That dream had taken shape at age four when he asked Jesus into his heart. Standing atop a kitchen chair, he prepared for ministry by "preaching" to his rapt siblings, then leaping onto them for special emphasis.

I felt guilty about my part in holding him back. After all, I shared in his call to pastor, too. In spite of my awful emotional - spiritual condition, the call lingered somewhere in the hovering mist.

The longer we lived our suburban lifestyle, the more we felt life slipping through our fingers. We got caught up in a keeping-up-with-the-Joneses syndrome, along with our competitive neighbors. It chafed at us, but we slid ever deeper into its yawning jaws.

We discussed returning to college every now and then. Considering the size of our family, our financial picture, and my enormous fear, the prospect seemed laughable. How would we make it? Dick abandoned the idea, but it gnawed at me. I thought about all the millionaires who would surely take pleasure in putting a bright, young, deserving man of Dick's sincerity through school. Since I knew no millionaires, I considered secretly placing an ad in the newspaper reading: "Wanted: sponsor for family man, called of God, desiring to complete school." Thank God I never did that, for He took care of it in His own good time without any help from me.

When Shellie was two years old, I decided to take the first step toward getting Dick back in school. I placed a different kind of ad, without his knowledge, to rent our home. When he dragged in from work, that night, I cheerfully announced that everything was set; the house had been rented, he could go to college for the fall term, and all was well. I would take care of the packing.

When he regained his composure, we talked about the importance of him finishing his education. It was decided that we would indeed head for Illinois as soon as possible. How? We didn't get that far.

The week after lease papers on our home were signed, we discovered a fourth child was on the way. Aborting our hastily made plans, we rented a house in East Detroit until the lease expired on our own, then returned home once more defeated.

During our time in East Detroit, we lost our spiritual moorings. Lonely, needy, embarrassed, and discouraged, we spent more and more Sundays home by ourselves. There wasn't a church that could hold our attention, so we just pulled in.

We unloaded the van at our house one month before David was born. The day he arrived, all three of the other children came down with measles. Mom filled the gap during my hospital stay, and warned her charges not to play outside in the sun. When she found evidence (wilted dandelions) hidden on their closet floor, she gave up on warnings and bought three pairs of sunglasses. A few miles away, David spent his first week of life with my sister-in-law until the measles passed. In spite of their spotty faces, his siblings looked very happy to be on home turf.

We made a sweet discovery shortly after returning home. A neighbor invited us to visit her church, which turned out to be just what the doctor ordered for our struggling family. Before long, we had joined the church and its choir.

Choir practice was our big night out. We got a babysitter so Dick and I could sing the music that had so captivated us in our youth. It was the highlight of my week; a good break from screaming at kids during the day and screaming at demons during the night. The enemy still intruded into my dreams, but there was a bright spot in the long, long tunnel of depression, if only on Tuesday nights.

Dick was enjoying his new singing opportunity, but by then he was losing his grip, doing things against his conscience to supposedly celebrate a round of golf after work. Severe anxiety closed in on him at night. Sometimes he felt like the top of his head would blow off from inner pressure. One morning at 5:00 a.m. he asked me to take him to the emergency room before he exploded. My neighbor gave a sleepy consent to check on the children and I drove Dick to the hospital, wondering which of us was worse off.

The doctor administered a shot to quiet him, saying he would likely sleep all day. A few hours later he was driving around the countryside wide awake, trying to figure things out. He insisted on driving to prove he still had control of something, if only a car. We agreed that something had to change, but we were unsure of what, or how.

Curious neighbors and our parents probed for answers. I explained that Dick had been working too hard too long. They bought that, knowing he was seldom home. I knew better, though. The root of his problem went deep into his spirit where failures of the past and fear of an empty future lay stuck beyond his reach. Ah, yes…

> The cry of the world
> Is to be fulfilled,
> Not knowing it cannot be;
> For to be fulfilled
> Has a spiritual root,
> And the root
> Is what feeds the tree.

He was tasting of the Godless world, denying the cry of his heart. Something had to give.

One life-changing evening, we went out on the town with one of Dick's co-workers and his wife. They were "swingers." I was not too excited about swinging with them, but going to a ski lodge for dinner without kids had a strong appeal. It was still hard to be with people, so I just listened and tried not to look as uneasy as I felt. Getting Dick out of the house for relaxation seemed a good thing. I could put up with some discomfort in exchange for a special outing.

When we got to the lodge, the man ordered a round of drinks. I wasn't a drinker, but played the part. Whatever was ordered for me quickly left me with double vision. As we made our way out, I finally understood why drinkers are referred to as "tipsy." I didn't see why liquor was touted as being "relaxing and enjoyable" by our friends. I couldn't wait to get home. But home wasn't in the plan quite yet.

The couple, who apparently knew all the night spots in Detroit, drove to three more places. Amplified hard rock, flashing lights, and scantily-costumed barmaids weren't my idea of fun. Mom always said I was a prude.

On the way home, I began thinking how crazy the whole evening had been. What a waste! Why were we hanging around those places trying to be somebody we weren't? What was ahead for us in such a life? A lifetime of playing social games in order to be part of the "in" crowd? We were going home feeling incredibly empty, considering how much time and money we had invested.

Dick's co-worker was boozed to sleep, so his wife drove. They appeared to have rehearsed the routine many times. I thought of Dick and me and determined I would never make the same concession.

Home couldn't come into view soon enough. My eyes strained ahead to see how far we had to go. Suddenly, movement of a figure stumbling by the side of the road caught my attention.

Our headlights flashed on a staggering man, shirt in hand, covered with blood, motioning us to stop. I gasped, but the woman kept driving. Though there was no room for another passenger in the tiny VW bug, that wasn't what kept us from stopping. Three of us were scared, and one was stone drunk. It was safer not to get involved. Our driver's oblivious husband slept the rest of the way, while I painfully pondered the story of the Good Samaritan, which had taken root early in childhood. And the root is what feeds the tree.

The incident had taken place near our babysitter's home, so we described the scene to her after calling police to check it out. I was all knotted up inside. Nothing new, but those knots had a new feel.

Leslie, the babysitter, hadn't been gone long when she called sobbing. She said the man we had seen was her girlfriend's father. He had been shot five times. Not only had we passed by an injured person, we had passed someone Leslie knew! Sleep came slowly that night as I contrasted the ridiculous indulgences of the evening with our dormant call to serve God.

The next day we learned that the man we had seen was not the man Leslie knew. Rather, the man in our headlights had been robbed and beaten upon leaving a bar. He would be alright. Somehow, it was a relief. Strange relief!

Dick and I talked about our life. Where were we headed? Was this really the good life? Were the values (or lack of) we were buying into the ones we wanted to keep? If we were so uncomfortable with this lifestyle, what were we doing in it? Were we getting too locked in to Suburbia, U.S.A. to get out? What about God's call when we were younger?

Once upon a darksome night,
Beside a lonely road,
A blood-bathed man,
Without a word,
Pointed us t'ward God.

Immediately following that incident, we set gears in motion for changing the course of our lives. Dick talked to our new pastor about his abandoned dream of being a minister. With his assistance and blessing, Dick began a home study course which would qualify him for a local preacher's license. He then entered night school to chop away at college classes as well. He was back in the saddle again.

Within six months we received a call to take a student pastorate in northern Lower Michigan. I was thrilled. Dick would finally be doing his heart's desire, and a total change might help me emotionally. I began packing a month ahead of schedule, enjoying the bare walls of the home we would leave behind for a second time.

Dick wrestled with how to break the news to his company. He had been there nine years, and was moving up the ladder. They had been good to him, allowing countless emergency trips home when I was at my worst. There was also the fear of ridicule as he recalled our last feeble and unsuccessful attempt to return to school.

Finally he worked up nerve to announce his plan. We hoped they would allow him to finish out his last two weeks so our finances would hold up until we got on the church payroll. If they were angry, perhaps they'd just tell him to leave immediately. Then what would we do?

Our wildest imaginings were unnecessary. The response of his bosses was unexpectedly warm and affirming. Not only his superiors, but many co-workers congratulated Dick on his decision. They were genuinely happy for him.

A couple of farewell parties were thrown by the company in our honor. Amidst gifts and smiles and congratulations, we spied an unmistakable longing in men's eyes as they talked about it "taking a lot of guts to do what you're doing." They knew what it meant to be locked in, wanting out. We didn't feel particularly gutsy, just drawn back to a way we knew we had to go.

It would be rough going financially. Dick would be attending college half time and pastoring two country churches half time. Income would be drastically cut. I had no job skills, or desire to work outside the home, what with four young children to care for. A second reality was my still-present fear of being out in the big, mean world.

I'd witnessed the financial pinch of Dick's family, and heard unbelievable tales of hardship from their parsonage past, so I braced for a life of poverty. Taking a kind of twisted delight in facing it, I bought a book titled "101 Ways to Fix Hamburger." We would likely never see a steak again. Surviving the rigors of parsonage life and living on a meager salary stimulated some unexpected excitement. But the reality of it all concerned us. What if there really wasn't enough to go around?

While making mental preparations for a hard financial transition, we also braced ourselves to live in a ramshackle, run-down house. To our surprise, we found a lovely, new, spacious ranch style home awaiting us. A sneak preview of our living quarters added to the joy of our approaching move.

His last day at work, Dick's bosses called him into the office. The President and Vice-President of the company were there. Pointing to an empty chair, they motioned a rather nervous employee to sit down. Their facial expressions gave no indication as to the purpose of the meeting. Maybe they just wanted to say a formal, private "good-bye." Instead, they announced their intention to support him through the rest of his education, both college and seminary; a minimum of four and a half years.

Their investment in his future would be to the tune of $200 per month, no strings attached. It was their way of blessing our move and God's way of providing our needs. Tears trickled from Dick's eyes as he told me how the "locked-in" men wanted to invest in him. I recalled the ad I never placed:

> "Wanted: Sponsor for family man,
> called of God,
> desiring to complete school."

We were keenly aware of the rightness of our decision, but largely unaware of the Hand of God in things. That came later.

FOUR

On The Move

February of 1966 marked a new phase of our tempestuous journey. As I followed the U-Haul truck in our family car, years of heaviness lightened with every passing mile. I sang at the top of my lungs, feeling like a bird set free. My kiddies must have sensed something big was happening, what with a two hour concert as introduction to our new life.

Arriving in tiny Sterling, Michigan was unlike any other move we'd made. Folks appeared from all corners of town and countryside to help us unload. When the job was finished, one of the farm families invited the six of us to join them for dinner. It was the first taste of what would prove to be enduring hospitality and friendships.

Home-grown buttered corn, high loaves of hot, homemade bread, beef from their own herd (cooked to perfection), and dessert that only a woman of Mennonite heritage can produce, welcomed our tired, hungry, happy family. It felt so good to leave the past in the past. Embracing an unknown, but God-chosen future, we went to bed that night feeling we were "home."

Within a matter of days, I was promoted to an uninvited position: expert parent. Inquiries began coming in as to how to raise children. It seemed that mine appeared to be such good cherubs. People didn't realize how little I knew about mothering. How quickly their illusions about me and my children would be shattered! It didn't take long for the natural unveiling to take place. My older boys went into motion before I could dream up the least advice about perfect parenting.

Steve and Jim exercised their sassy jaws to town bullies, and secretly collected beer bottles to sell for cigarettes, which they smoked in the hayloft of a barn belonging to the parishioners who fed us our first day in town. The boys also rode the family's cows when no one was looking. Candy bars from a church member's market found their way into the boys' jeans pockets, too…unpaid for, of course.

Inquiries about child rearing came to a screeching halt one snowy winter morning. I had already taken the children to one of our churches for morning worship. Trying to be the model preacher's family, I took them to the second church's service, also.

Things were going quite well. All four children filed in behind me. We resembled a mother duck with her four ducklings following behind. We filled the better part of a pew in front. My husband asked everyone to close their eyes and repeat the Lord's Prayer with him. About midway through the prayer, four year old David pierced the somber Sabbath moments with an angry outburst: "I'm sick and tired of church!" he yelped.

With gaping jaw and eyes popped open, I spun my head in the direction of that fed-up little boy. There stood otherwise docile David Bradley North, tie dangling from his clenched fist, standing on the pew with his freshly ironed white shirt unbuttoned all the way to his pants. As casually as a frazzled mother could, I buttoned him up and fastened his tie, feeling he should be thankful it was a clip-on type, as opposed to a Bolo.

After that day, double church attendance was no longer mandatory for my brood, and questions pertaining to parenting ceased. Rather, moms relaxed and let their kids be like mine…just kids who didn't always relish sitting through sermons and songs.

As lovely as the people were in our first parish, they couldn't negate the problems that we had, to my dismay, dragged along with us. I grew increasingly fearful, imagining all sorts of terrible things happening. Adding to my long-standing neurosis were the added burdens of being a preacher's wife. People had huge expectations. Our church families were kind and understanding, but there were watchful eyes and critical comments that came to my attention from the community.

I didn't like going to meetings out of obligation, nor playing the role of "together" preacher's wife. I was 29, and anything but together. Spoken and unspoken demands on my time made for an unhappy little lady.

Dick had his own anxieties. Whatever else he wanted, his highest goal was to be a good, effective preacher. He toiled with his college load, working long hours on sermon preparation. His extremely uptight pattern of preparation for Sundays made me dread Saturday nights.

All week long, he pored over books and articles, gleaning just the right material for a dynamic sermon. Saturday he wrote the material, and after I went to bed he typed it up. While pulling up the covers, I closed my eyes and stuffed my ears to endure hours of him pecking on the metal monster. Any error made meant another wad of paper sailing through the air, pinging in the wastebasket.

Sunday mornings, before the birds awoke, Dick slipped out of the house, crossed the yard to the church, and rehearsed his sermon. Once. Twice. Three times. In spite of good material, his sermons were void of power. We both knew it.

Things weren't squaring. The whole sermon process was painful from beginning to end. I wondered how long he could handle such unrealistic expectations of himself. He frustrated me with endless rehearsals. Not only were the kids and I trying to live out an uncomfortable role, Dick was increasingly tense about his new identity. Resentments grew as I found each of us rubbing up against those expectations. Making concessions in order to be liked reminded me of appeasing Jerry, the snowball tyrant.

Regardless of the many pressures, we thoroughly enjoyed our rural flock. Life in the country was healing. One of the most beautiful scenes imprinted on our minds and hearts is drawn from an afternoon in autumn, 1966. We loved to drive along dirt back roads that wound through the forest near Sterling where herds of deer fed in the cornfields.

One special day, we got out of the car and walked into a colorful grove of trees. Fall had torched sugar maples into breathtaking red-oranges. Surrounding the vibrant hues stood a grove of trees clad in glowing yellow-gold gowns. Like billowy evening gowns, they danced with each breath of breeze, radiating like waves at an ocean sunset. Only distant chirps of birds and the slight rustle of falling leaves broke the golden silence. Just when we most needed refreshing, something real to touch in the midst of our role-playing existence, God gave us a beauty bath!

Meanwhile, back at the ranch, I groped for the meaning of my life - a real identity. From the pit of depression, I asked some serious questions, not really expecting answers.

Who am I? And why?
From where does this soul come,
And where does it go?
For what purpose?
I struggle to "become."
Become what? And for whom?
Shall I forever wonder,
And never know?
Can I not find myself
In THIS life,
And thrive in its present tense?
Must ultimate joy
Be ever before me
In unattainable reach?
I long to know myself,
To answer the question marks,
And find a reasonable rest here and now.
Does anyone know how?

Dick and I made a trip to see the seminary in January of '67. We were determined to keep our family on campus, which was possible due to the generosity of Dick's former employer.

Campus apartments were small. We would have to cram six of us into space one-third of what we had enjoyed in the parsonage. We would have a tiny kitchen, small living room, two upstairs bedrooms and bath, and two small closets for storage. A hide-a-bed would suffice for Dick and me for the next three years. We took it, again with a rise of anticipation, mixed with apprehension.

The campus was lovely, even in the dead of winter: rolling farm hills, magnificent trees, a brook which emptied under a wooden bridge into a pond populated with ducks and geese, and Georgian style buildings, blending gracefully with tranquil surroundings.

We met with a few administrative people. Students were gone for the weekend, so there wasn't much activity. The dull, blustery day didn't diminish the feeling that my answer was there. I knew in my heart that this place would make all the difference. With that assurance, I returned to the far north and held on for many more months.

After only sixteen months at our new assignment, my husband finished his college classes and made preparation to enter a seminary in Ohio. We had planned to stay in Michigan another year, but Dick's urge to finish school was strong. We dug in for the long haul. Leaving the friendly people of Sterling would be hard, but we had stalled God for nine years. It was time to go.

June was bustin' out all over when we made a temporary move to a small town in another area of Michigan. It was another two-church appointment. Dick would again attend classes all summer while the children and I held down the parsonage fort until August.

The summer appointment had such a fleeting feel to it that I didn't bother to unpack my pans. They stayed in an open box alongside the stove. No floor coverings or window shades were provided in the two story parsonage, which was located on the main street of town. Floors had been covered with a layer of brown butcher paper cut in yard-wide strips.

We stared in disbelief at the prospect of a summer with paper floors. With a trip to the nearest shopping center we splurged on a 9 x 12 foot area rug for one room, but my nerves grew ragged trying to protect the strange paper "rugs" from six sets of active feet. I finally gave up.

Not long after taking up residence in the small town, I got wind of some discontent among townsfolk. I seldom went out of the house, except to get the mail a couple of times. It was hot. We had no air conditioning. It made sense to wear shorts. The sight of a preacher's wife in shorts at the local post office sent shock waves through town. Shorts were not acceptable attire for me. Retreating to the safe inner sanctum of "home", I counted the days until our move - like I counted down for Christmas as a child.

Shortly (pardon the pun) after the shorts incident, I learned that strolling through the house at night in my bathrobe was giving someone else fits. With no shades on the windows, I had inadvertently set off an alarm in whoever was watching from nearby. We requested the church to buy some shades, since we were temporary. The church board was sufficiently disturbed to invest in shades, no drapes. Two months to go. Terrible dreams marched into that house. One had to do with a group of people who were beating up on an invalid in a wheelchair. It took place in front of our house. I screamed for them to stop, but no one listened. No one helped.

I woke up sweating, in a state of terror. I was the invalid. People were beating me senseless with silly criticisms and unfair expectations. I, too, screamed for help. But no one came. That's because my screaming was done inside, where no one could hear. Oh, to be where it was safe – wherever that might be. I remembered the previous unexplainable assurance about the seminary, pulled the new shades one last time, dreamed one last ugly dream there, and rose to a new day, a new adventure, a new home.

FIVE

Overcome To Overcomer

Children of seminary families swarmed from all corners of the campus when our U-Haul truck backed up to apartment B-5. Kids don't take long to break down barriers, so our boys and daughter disappeared with their new friends within just a few minutes. A few students lumbered across the grassy apron in front to help us unload. By nightfall we had wound up the first day of what would become three of the most exhilarating, challenging years of our lives.

Dick had to return to the Michigan church we had just left to preach one last time, since the new pastor wouldn't arrive for another week. Staying alone at night normally scared the wits out of me, but this night was different. As he drove down the long, winding driveway in the dark of night, I felt totally at peace. Rain was pelting the porch roof outside my window, creating a sound of welcome. I curled up and enjoyed my aloneness until falling into the first relaxed, dreamless sleep in years. My fears took a brief, but real, rest.

When Monday arrived, Dick entered eagerly into a new routine of full time studies and weekend pastoring. I thought he was happy. Within a week, however, such intense anxieties beset him that he sought out the school psychiatrist, Dr. Baumgartner. Dr. B. had originally intended to become a medical missionary, but somewhere along the line he jumped the track to psychiatry. He also had a seminary degree, and ordination papers. He provided individual and group counseling to students and their family members on a part time basis.

Dr. B. immediately discerned that Dick's struggles were not confined to him. I was invited to talk with the doc, also. My negative past counseling experience wasn't worth writing home about, but I felt a curlous mixture of anxiety and anticipation at the thought of meeting him.

Everything about my thirty year old body suggested very poor self-image. I, as usual, was overly self-conscious about my appearance, having long since quit caring how I looked. "Bad hair days" were daily fare, and extra pounds had accumulated while stuffing myself with comfort food. Oh, so what? Nobody knew I was alive anyway.

Early September breezes blew through the pines as I walked down the winding walk to Dr. B's office. My tap on the door summoned a tall, dark, handsome gentleman who didn't resemble a textbook therapist in the least. I thought I had the wrong room, but he invited me in; into his office, into his heart, into a whole, new, exciting, freeing world. Within the hour, I had hope.

Dr. B. fiddled with a dial on the window ledge. "Undoubtedly a tape recorder", I thought. He said the air conditioner needed adjusting. With an imperceptive blush, I admitted to myself that I was paranoid. Sometime during the hour, I decided Dr. B. could be trusted. He was real. He was my answer. I knew it in my bones. Dick would also find his answer there, but not without much upheaval and hard work.

Dr. B. was a continual surprise. That's what I liked about him. His unusual blend of uniqueness, vulnerability, compassion, musical giftedness, and incredible capacity for accurately discerning behaviors, as well as appropriate responses to them, made for a remarkable emotional journey.

The picture shouldn't be painted too rosy, though. His sensitivities and piercing perceptions didn't necessarily create a comfy environment. He had ways of pinching emotional nerves at the most embarrassing, unexpected times. But whether he praised or pinched, it was to my advantage to pay attention to his insights.

Observing Dr. B. in action, whether in groups or one-on-one, taught me a lot about letting myself be known. If he felt sad, he said so. Often open with his tears about something or other made me feel worthy of his trust. If something angered him, it came out in flashes of honest encounter, opening a door of opportunity for resolution. I learned, in his presence, how to appropriately respond to someone who shares deep feelings, and how to expose some of my own.

Dr. B. had the rare quality of seeing through to a person's core in a matter of minutes. That didn't always win him favor with everyone. He experienced his share of rejection; some didn't like his tears. Some didn't like his style. Others didn't like the freedom he enjoyed in being his unusual self. But others delighted in him, learned volumes about life from him, and got emotionally well as a result of knowing him. I was one of those. I related to him as if he was the Pied Piper, following his lead through three chaotic years. I followed because, somewhere in the deepest part of me, I knew he would lead me out of hell. That knowledge came from way down inside, where words aren't enough.

Before meeting Dr. B., I had felt suicidal for 12 years. It was sink or swim time, so I entered a student wives' therapy-oriented share group. Dick pursued separate counseling for his problems as I tackled mine in the group and one-on-one formats.

Dr. B. was co-leader of the group, sharing responsibilities with another professor. Tension was high as the group gathered, making communication nigh unto impossible for me. I'd been used to passively expressing myself via silences, tantrums, pouting, depression, and overdoses of pills. It would mean a complete about-face just to speak without going to pieces. I wasn't sure I knew how. Dr. B. would be there, so I risked it. He sat opposite me.

Anxiety walked into the room with about ten gals. I made an advance decision to observe, not participate, as did many others in the group. Being new on campus, none of us knew anyone. Tension peaked at the mere presence of a psychiatrist and counselor. What would that psychiatrist do to wring out of us what we didn't want to say? What sneaky methods would he use to expose our secrets? The tense silence was a giveaway that we were hiding a lot. But Dr. B. wasn't in the business of pulling emotional teeth, as we soon discovered.

The first session turned out to be a sweet surprise. Whatever negative things I expected to happen didn't. Something wonderful happened instead.

A young, newly married girl talked about her experience since arriving on campus. She and her student husband moved into the married student's dorm, a building designed like residence halls at colleges. The girl sadly stated that, although a lot of students and couples passed by their apartment, no one ever bothered to stop…even when the door was left open as an invitation to visit. Hers was a simple statement: she found it so "disappointing."

I waited for a response from someone. Surely anyone could see that she wasn't just disappointed; she was lonely. It seemed to glare from between the lines in neon lights. Surprisingly, neither co-leader responded. Dr. B. searched the faces of our group. Out of nowhere, I startled myself with my own voice. "You must feel very lonely with so many people passing right on past you."

She teared up and gave me that special look that said, "You understand." I wasn't aware of anything unusual in our interchange until one of the leaders very tenderly picked up on my comments. With his affirmation, he catapulted me into a brand new appreciation for my unrecognized sensitivities. I thought anyone could hear the real message behind the girl's words, but I was the only one who did. For the first time, I felt "smart"; like I had something of value inside. It was the first of many intriguing discoveries about *me*.

I immediately began "fixing up." First my hair, then my clothes. How could such a simple interchange make a person feel new? I got a job in the campus social room, where I could be part of campus life. It worked wonders, forcing my fearful personality to cross emotional boundaries it hadn't dared to explore until someone spotted hidden treasure I hadn't realized was there.

Becoming more involved and familiar with the wives' group, and continuing personal counseling with Dr. B., I soon broke out of my self-imposed prison, dropping former timidity for a strange, new boldness. As is so often the case with pendulums, they either swing too far one way or the other. I had swung from being an introverted fraidy cat to a vocal, aggressive, controversial figure in my little corner of the world. It felt great, and it hurt.

Like a bull in a china shop, I did my best to navigate through delicate situations to no avail. Crashing into, often wounding, people who had their own set of problems stacked a pile of regrets at my feet. At age thirty, I didn't yet know how to relate with those around me. I hoped others realized that I was suffering from growing pains. Some did. Some didn't.

During one particularly stormy group session, one gal reached her fill of me and told me so. I'd been good at dishing it out, but was still too thin-skinned to take criticism. Her words knocked all the props out from under me. I left the room embarrassed and crying. What was wrong with me now? I just didn't know how to behave any more. Someone was always getting hurt or insulted because of my amazing insights. Maybe I didn't have anything good inside after all. Most certainly, I should keep my mouth shut and let others do the relating. Forget personal potential and openness!

The counselor had called me "brutally honest" – as if that was a gift. Some gift! Did that mean that I would have to live dis-honestly in order to get along? Oh, who knew what anything meant? I wasn't very pleasant to be around since spreading my wings and feeling my oats. I hated to give up, and dreaded going on, somewhat like I felt when I set the field on fire years ago.

Classes had let out for the day. Hallways were empty, most lights turned out. I hunkered down in an unlit stairwell near Dr. B's office while the group continued without me. There, I cried like a little kid who had been caught in some mischief, and kicked out of the club, though it was I who slammed the door behind me.

When the group dispersed, and Dr. B. returned to his office to gather things up for his departure home, I left my place of reflection – my inner war zone – to intercept him. As I stepped through the doorway, into the hall, he didn't say a word; just dropped his coat, put his arms around me, and held on until my uncontrollable sobs subsided. As lovingly as anyone could, he held on through my snorts and sniffs, shaking and moaning. I felt like a little girl all troubled and lost and small. But he held on.

When I finally quit crying, I simply went home and thought about the gift of love I had received from the man who shared healing strength in a silent hug. At some level, I thought about God. How I wished He would hold me like that, not knowing He just had:

> To see love shine in human eyes
> And hear it in a human voice,
> To feel its strength in human hands,
> Must surely be the tend'rest part of God
> I'll ever know.

Although my counseling experience was not of a religious nature, I began using spiritual language and symbols in my poetry. The meaning of resurrection came clearer as I felt the death in me spring to life.

Early in therapy, I took a friend's baby for a walk in a field of newly mown grass. He was experiencing new things physically; I was experiencing new things emotionally. I marveled that a year old baby was doing something identical to me, a thirty year old mother of four, who was only then learning to walk in my relationships.

> A baby took a walk today
> And, tumbling in the grass,
> Quite by chance discovered Life…
> Afraid to trust, withdrew from it;
> Strange, unknown stuff!

His wide eyes studied as his fingers
Traced the blades,
Then looked up and searched my eyes
To see if it was safe.
Exploring once again,
His fear burst into sheer delight
As discovery took place,
Became a part of him,
And shone upon his face.

I made quick progress in counseling, unable to get enough of my new life. People commented on the apparent improvement in my attitude and appearance. At last, the changes weren't all bad. I really could get along with people. I even felt loved by a few.

When Christmas vacation came, Dick had put in a successful semester scholastically, and was dealing effectively with his struggles. I reveled in the agony and ecstasy of change.

At the turn of the new year, we went out with a campus couple. Pulling alongside another twosome who were stopped beside us at a red light, a bolt from the blue smacked me off my silver-lined emotional cloud. It was such a simple thing.

Our seminary friends launched into a negative tirade about the total strangers next to us because of their color. Being sensitive to the issue of racial prejudice, I flashed back to the invalid dream I'd had months earlier. How could someone who was preparing for ministry muster so much hatred for someone who was just plain being alive? It seemed so unfair.

I felt the same horror of being helpless. The brutalizing crowd in my dream was too big for me to handle. Why, they couldn't even hear me! Now I felt equally unable to help. The tide of racial prejudice was too big for one person to stop. I sank into a pit of depression that would require major work to overcome.

The depression wasn't created by our friends' remarks. It came because the issues of helplessness and human oppression hadn't yet been resolved within myself. The racial incident just brought my own fears and vulnerabilities to light again.

Sometimes seeing a child harshly treated, or boys fighting, triggered enormous hopelessness. I kept recalling the boys in my sixth grade class who brutalized their victim, then intimidated those of us who wanted to do right. Not doing right resulted in us doing wrong. I couldn't make a difference in the scheme of things then, and I couldn't make a difference in this situation. Feeling overwhelmed with hopelessness for the human race, and being a part of it, I despaired about my lack of ability to cope with life.

I stood at the ironing board the following day as if paralyzed. Following that emotional earthquake I could do no more than stare at the shirt or blouse awaiting a press. Preparing meals for my family was so taxing I could hardly lift a fork to my mouth. It more often dropped to my plate as I stared off into space. I quit talking for the most part. Walking room to room took all I had. It felt like I was in some kind of shock. It was wintertime. As in my ninth year, it looked like a long one.

When classes resumed, I called for an appointment with Dr. B. Sensing the depth of my despondency, he prescribed an anti-depressant and set up another appointment for the following day. I knew it was serious, for the campus closed down weekends. Saturday was his day off, and it was a long drive from his home to the school. He said something about flowers being there; I just couldn't see them yet. But I would. It was impossible to imagine flowers in that black hour, but the symbol reached me. I trusted Dr. B. with my life, but I didn't trust my ability to ever see flowers again.

I gave the prescription to my husband. He went to fill it while I went home to care for my kindergarten son and a neighbor's boy. Trudging upstairs, I looked in the mirror once more, glanced down at the children (who were unaware of the storm), looked at the full bottle of aspirin on the counter top, once again told myself I was crazy, and swallowed them all.

The world is black.
I cannot see the flowers.
I am alone.
Loneliness is black indeed.

The note I left behind simply said, "I'm getting out." While the children played, I slipped out the back door, crossed the yard to another residential unit, and let myself in the basement storage area. Locking the door behind me, I crawled onto a shelf in our designated storage bin and waited for the unknown. Whatever result might come from a heavy dose of lowly aspirin didn't really matter.

Being January, it grew dark early. That fit my frame of mind. Smells of food cooking upstairs, the noisy din of families chattering, scolding, arguing and thumping toys, fell on my senses. I wondered if anyone was happy anywhere. Prepared to sleep it off or die, I leaned back on the wooden slats.

Instead of falling into a deep sleep, a relentless loud ringing filled my head. I got jumpier by the minute. After several hours of restlessness, I left my hiding place. Walking back to the apartment, I felt like I was lifting a load of lead with every step. Acute toxemia does that. I walked through my tiny kitchen, past the couple who had been with us that unsettling night. They were there feeding my family of four. Without speaking, I plodded upstairs and flopped on my bed.

When Dick returned from filing a missing person's report, he took one look at me and asked how many pills I'd taken. After a quick call to Dr. B., he called our family doctor and drove me to the emergency room. By then I was having trouble breathing, so we opened the car windows, letting January's frigid air blow in. It didn't help. My system was paying a high price for my despairing actions.

A nurse who had no patience for the likes of me ushered me into the treatment area. She said my doctor had gone home for dinner, having just finished treating "another one just like you." She gave me some liquid to drink, dunked my head over a basin and left me to heave it out.

Having wretched long enough to clean my stomach out and satisfy the angry nurse, I was led upstairs and put to bed. My head felt weighted down and my eyes couldn't hold themselves open, in spite of the fact that I was far from being sleepy. The jitters lasted two days, along with severe ringing in my ears. Nobody asked, so I didn't tell. I figured they ought to know. Regression.

All through the night my husband wandered the halls, peeking in, squeezing my hand. I hated him being there. I hated a lot of things. Especially me. But he stayed.

The ringing in my ears hadn't yet diminished when Dr. B. came to visit the next day. I was ashamed, but relieved that he understood my screamless scream for help. Without the clutter of words, he understood.

Arrangements were made for my transfer to a private psychiatric hospital where Dr. B. worked half time. Monday morning, following a heavy snowstorm, I gathered up the red roses Dick had given me and stepped outside. On the way to the car, I watched their velvet petals wilt in the cold air. It was in keeping with everything else.

An exquisite snowscape greeted us as we crossed a little bridge at the hospital's entrance. Snow draped trees and bushes, fences and posts. Intricate snow-weave designs on bridge railings created lattice work resembling a fairyland. I was grateful for the serene, secluded setting, yet felt a rising anxiety as I reported at the desk for admittance.

My teeth chattered so vigorously I was embarrassed. The chill shuddering through me had nothing to do with the cold day. I was scared – chilled to the bone with fear. What was ahead? How would they treat me? Would I be safe?

I did my best to answer interview questions between my uncontrollable clacking teeth. Soon the ordeal was over, but the shaking continued until I was escorted to the Lodge, a minimum security facility.

The Lodge was a big, old, two-story house where most patients could come and go with few restrictions. A friendly nursing staff stayed on site around the clock. I was closely observed because of the pill episode, but enjoyed more freedom than I expected. I was glad to be under someone else's care, being weary of trying to hold myself together. It wasn't working anyway. Maybe this lovely, snow-clad place would offer some peace and healing.

Sleep rarely happened during my hospitalization. I often gazed out the second story window at night, while my roommates slept. Sugary mounds of snow sparkled in the moonlight as people drove past the grounds, on their way to waiting families. Homes which had glittered so recently with Christmas lights housed people who lived unaware of a lady named Pat. Pat longed for something more.

> Where are the answers
> For a searching heart?
> A soul that's daily discontent?
> Strength in one's self is much too frail.
> It withers in the heat of life;
> The hurtful time.
> I shall forever be alone.
> A part of me cannot be free,
> For loneliness imprisons me.
> It changes trust to fear
> And warmth to cold.
> The skipping heart
> Becomes a broken vessel
> Unable to contain
> What's good and fine and real.
> How sheltered one must keep one's self
> To miss the pain.
> It's safer not to feel.

It didn't take long for the stark realities of confinement to set in. Though there was an illusion of freedom at the Lodge, I was escorted to and from all activities elsewhere. Doors were locked after me, evoking heightened anxiety about being mistreated or in danger. Unless the "keeper of the keys" was around, there would be no escaping abuse or fire. Of course, the key person *was* always around.

There's a humiliation that attends confinement. I found myself among a segment of society that couldn't manage itself. Like little kids who need a mom to give directions and set limits, patients at the Lodge required constant supervision. The most degrading part of my hospitalization, however, was sanding a wooden bowl - occupational therapy prescribed by Dr. B.

Day after day I sanded that meaningless hunk of wood, never seeming to make any discernable progress. I hated the job, and I hated the bowl. Soon, I bordered on hating Dr. B. for assigning me to the sanding detail. Why should I be given such an unfulfilling, aggravating task, when other people were doing fun, creative projects within the same four walls? Dr. B. knew I had a creative bent. Sanding wood was like a slap in the face. What is the purpose of a slap in the face to someone who is already depressed, withdrawn, down on herself?

After a few days of silently fuming about "bowl duty", I marched into Dr. B's office and gave him an earful. "It's boring, meaningless, and aggravating! Why do I have to do this?" He grinned and wrote out a new order for something more rewarding.

Without knowing it, I had taken an important first step toward health. Verbalizing my negative feelings, as opposed to swallowing a bunch of pills in protest, pleased the man who knew it must happen before I could ever crawl out of the pit of depression. So simple. So small. But small beginnings lead to great things.

Two and one half weeks later I was released. There had been a dramatic change in attitude toward my husband and children. After finding acceptance for expression of my honest feelings about the bowl, I ventured into the arena of marriage. Surprisingly, I found it safe to talk out loud about things I had carried inside for years. The desire to give, give, give, mushroomed. It was good to be home.

Into these depths, somehow,
May light flood in
And shine on endless

Fields of flowers.
I know they're there.
If I become renewed,
So I can thrive in this
World's brilliance,
The intensity of life
Will not destroy me,
But, rather, create me daily.

Counseling resumed on a weekly basis at the seminary. I re-entered the wives' group with the goal to better understand myself and learn new ways of dealing with life.

In April of 1968, a group of seminary students and spouses were offered the opportunity of touring Haiti mission sites at quite a reasonable price. I needed to prove some things. Going off on my own, away from the predictability and safety of home, would be a first. Feeling too dependent on Dick, I decided to go. And undecided. And decided. And undecided.

The driver of our little group of five became so exasperated with my indecision that he obviously hoped I'd stay home, but I was still loading and unloading at midnight. Changing old familiar ways wasn't easy.

At the crack of dawn, I surprised myself (and everyone else) by taking my place in the back seat and waving good-bye to my family. With every passing mile, I felt a rush of panic. There was no turning back. By the end of the first day's travel, I had slipped into a quiet crying jag. The girl beside me patted my hand. The others thought I was catching cold.

By the time we reached the motel, my anxiety was out of control. I called Dick to tell him I would have to take a train home. It was like old times; and just knowing I could get out relieved my mind. I settled in for the long journey. When morning came, I left for Florida with four bewildered fellow travelers.

Various church families met our entourage to house us for the night. A widow lady with two toy poodles and one real Cadillac chauffeured my friend and me to her home. She clucked to her dogs like they were people as we wound through the streets of Ft. Lauderdale. In between endearments to Baby and Missy, she announced that Dr. Martin Luther King, Jr. had just been shot and killed. My friend and I, seated in back, stared at each other in disbelief.

The lady hissed her contempt for Dr. King, saying he had gotten what he deserved. While she explained her position as faithful treasurer of the women's group at church, I tried doing some mental addition. With math never being my strong suit, I failed to make any of it come out right.

Unable to sleep in the lady's luxurious guest bed, I tossed and turned all night. How could dogs get such humane treatment and a human get such inhumane treatment? Not too long before the incident, I would have handled the disillusionment with a bottle of pills. I must have made some progress with Dr. B., I thought, because I was just plain mad. I regretted not taking the train home. If only I hadn't been brave enough to change my mind and step into the unknown.

There I was, in a strange place, with riots threatening to break out. Come morning I would fly for the first time in an awful winged monstrosity over an ocean of water to a dictatorship country! If riots, plane, ocean, dictator government, and polluted drinking water didn't get me, I'd be a winner.

A week later, I returned to the states just that - a winner! I had mingled with strangers, conversed with foreigners, dealt with every shade of fear imaginable, and discovered that I could actually survive in unusual circumstances without my husband. What a milestone! Just knowing that made me want to be with him. Finally, I felt like a woman instead of a little girl.

Classes dismissed for the summer, but arrangements were made for me to continue counseling. Sessions were scheduled at the hospital where I had stayed in January. Although we were making much progress, enormous personal changes were creating much-needed upheaval between Dick and me. Communication was our most difficult problem. In spite of some spurts of progress, sharing feelings came hard. Reverting to old patterns of silences and tantrums came easily.

Dick and I stopped seeing Dr. B. together after the first year. We had become too competitive, unable to fully appreciate each other's gains and breakthroughs. I wanted Dr. B's full attention, and a minimum of pressure from Dick to change. The day we broke our pattern of separate counseling was a terrible, yet important day, as I had to face myself in a most painful way.

Our competitiveness was at a peak. Dick insisted that we see Dr. B. together. All kinds of resentment surfaced, but I agreed. As we were sitting in Dr. B's office, trying to begin a difficult session, I did some manipulating to get Dick out. Somehow, I convinced them both that we should be seen separately. As Dick started outside to wait his turn, I grinned like a Cheshire cat that had caught a mouse. Got my way.

Dr. B. saw the little smile of victory. His dark brown eyes flashed anger directly at me. His face held a mirror before me which reflected my selfish image; an image I couldn't tolerate. I blew up. He was supposed to be on *my* side. I ran out of the office (de-je-vous), screaming at both of them to get lost. No more therapy for me! I stormed past the secretary and waited in the car.

After a flurry of unsuccessful attempts by both of them to persuade me back into the office, we left. Dick fumed all the way home. I bristled like a porcupine. As soon as I got home, I called my parents in Michigan and asked them to come and get me. Later that night they arrived to try some negotiation, but I was dug in.

I laid on the hard bedroom floor in the boy's room, but sleep didn't come until about 5 a.m. Dick walked the campus all night. Early in the morning I dozed off only to awaken with a suffocating feeling. The weight of the situation manifested in a dream. In it, a heavy weight perched on my chest. I woke up gasping for air, knowing it wasn't a breathing problem, but a life-crisis.

A few hours later I took the two youngest children, ten dollars, a lot of anger, and headed for Michigan. What I thought I could do with two kids and ten dollars, I'll never know. Anger does strange things to reason. And God moves in mysterious ways, His wonders to perform.

TURNING POINT

I was pushed
That bright and sunny day
So far beyond my limits
That I had to run away and hide.
I gathered up my younger two
And left the others with their dad.
The five hour drive
Left many miles between us,
Symbolic of where we were
In our marriage.
Every mile felt like a stab.
Jimmy's sad, sad face
Kept reappearing in my mind.
He said, as I was leaving,
"Mom, my throat hurts."
I wondered how his throat was,

And if he'd really hurt
Anymore without me
Than he would with me,
Or if he'd hurt as much.
The thought that he'd
Be better off without me
Wasn't any comfort.
I knew, deep down,
He needed me,
And wondered why
It was so hard
For me to let him.
He was catcher
For the Little League team,
A tiger of a ball player.
Steve, his brother,
Was pitcher for the same team;
A tiger, too.
They had a game scheduled
The next night
And I thought,
"Oh, GOD, I wish
I could be there.
I wish we weren't all
So broken up
In little pieces,
Hurting so much ourselves
That we can't help each other,
Or have some fun together."
Mom said,
"You want to go back?
We haven't gone too far
To turn back."
I shook my head "no",
Knowing if I spoke
I'd fall apart.
Shellie tried to smile
As Grandma threw her caring glances.
She tried to be a good girl,
Wondering, I suppose,

How her world had crashed so fast
And why it had to crash at all.
It was painful watching
As she tried to hide the fear
A child must feel
When life is suddenly chaotic.
I thought of Steve…
If he'd pitch his best
And keep an eye on Jim
And know I hadn't left him there
Because I loved him less;
And if he'd know,
At his tender age,
It had to be this way
For now
So his dad wouldn't be alone
And he and Jim could play ball
And not have their summer fun
Ruined because of me.
I thought of Dick…
How awful it had been
Trying to rebuild
Our shattered dream.
How much he meant to me before;
How angry I was now
That he had pressured me.
We drove for hours.
I knew before arriving
That I couldn't stay.
I grieved for not only
The missing parts
I'd left behind,
But for the part of me
I knew I must now bid farewell,
For it was time to get rid of
Some things in ME.
Some games.
Some selfishness.
Some fear.
But what would there be

To take the place of old, inadequate,
Yet comfortable, ways?
I walked in the field
Behind the house
While Mom and Dad went for
A supply of groceries;
Alone,
So aware of my
Aloneness.
The flowers,
Weeds,
Clouds,
Grass,
Sky,
Everything in sight,
Looked distant,
Desolate.
I felt separate from myself
And those I loved,
Unclear about my purpose for living.
Afraid that I would surely die that day
If I did not return myself *to* myself,
Heal my broken parts,
My family,
And build a new life.
In the clarity
Of that moment,
And in the strength
Of decision to change,
I picked up the phone and dialed.
Dick answered.
I said, "Hi! It's me. How is Jim's throat?
I have to come home. Will you come and get us?"
He said, "Sure."
I told my folks what I had to do…
Apologized for the 600 miles
They drove that day
To help me out of something
Too big for me,
And set my heart toward home.

The next night,
Our dynamic duo
Won their game.
We hit a home run, too;
The six of us,
Together.

Dr. B. once said that until a person hurts enough, he will not change; hurt has the power to catapult a person into action. This insight was confirmed by a surgeon who unwittingly shared the same truth in a hospital waiting room one evening. It was our last year of seminary – a semester packed with one health crisis after another.

Our little girl had just undergone emergency surgery for Primary Peritonitis. The doctor had a brief break in activity, and chatted with us while we waited to see Shellie. Suddenly, terrible moans spilled into the waiting area from behind emergency room curtains, where the doctor had just finished treating several accident victims.

He was in a talkative, casual mood, so when I commented on how stressful it must be to see people in such pain, he jumped at the chance to respond. His eyes sparkled like someone about to describe a favorite hobby.

To my astonishment, the doctor enthusiastically said how pleased he was to hear the groans. My startled expression prompted him to explain that he was most concerned when the patient came in silent, unconscious, unmoving. In other words, as long as a person is alert enough to hurt, there's hope! I knew it was not only true of the human body, but emotions, relationships, and behaviors.

Later, I would know that this insight springs from God Himself. Man had just applied spiritual truth (pained to repentance) to other areas of life.

Time and again during the course of three years of on-again, off-again counseling, I had experienced being pained to change. No sooner did I correct one fault than I'd see another, wrangling with self until the "thing" relinquished to healthier ways. Over and over, round and round, me with me, old to new.

So it went day in and day out, until finally I could look in the mirror and take pleasure in what I saw and who I had become. I didn't know who Jacob was then, but when I later read of his wrestling match with the angel, I felt I had another brother, the only difference being I didn't have a limp as evidence of the battle, just a big smile on my face and spring in my step.

SIX

The Gift of Dreams

We had been living in our seminary apartment for one year when a groaning U-Haul truck backed up to the adjoining apartment. As our new neighbor stepped down from the silver-orange beast, I got the impression he had been miscast for the part. A more natural scene would have had him disembarking from a covered wagon, complete with desert dust, ala John Wayne.

But "Rick" was his handle. Rick stood well over six feet tall, and sported a smile which perfectly matched his warm, southern drawl, fresh from Tennessee. When he walked, even in wide open spaces, he leaned as if there were rafters or door jambs to be avoided overhead. He lumbered gently, spoke softly, and laughed easily, treating those around him with a certain tenderness. The strength he emanated was the quiet kind.

Jane, pulling in close behind Wayne's counterpart in a stuffed VW "bug", could have starred in her own movie for she too was striking; tall, slender, and very attractive with her long, dark hair curled nicely by Mother Nature. Her voice revealed a trace of shyness. More predominant, as time went by, was her enthusiasm for the little things in life - whether watching an ant colony conduct business as usual in a crack of the sidewalk, or introducing us deprived northerners to "black-ahhhed-payeez."

A utility room with shared laundry facilities separated my kitchen from Jane's. If kitchen doors were left ajar, we could carry on a conversation while puttering around. Eager to settle into their new place, the Kirchoffs hurriedly unpacked boxes of belongings, tossing the empties outside "our" laundry room. Scrawled across one box were the words "Chris's Things." Within a few days, Rick's mother arrived with her arms full of red-haired, bombastic, eighteen month old Christopher Paul Kirchoff.

During the following two years, our little neighbor managed to slip from his "house" into ours on many occasions, via the shared utility room. As I sank into a nice afternoon nap on Shellie's bed, a thunderous discord from the organ downstairs nearly shot me through the roof! Hurrying downstairs, I found the young maestro hammering his little fists on the ivories, clad only in his underwear and a sheepish grin – typically Chris.

There were many children Chris's age living on campus at that time. The training pants set engaged in daily demolition derbies with their tricycles, racing up and down sidewalks, bumping into each other and squealing like little pigs. Parents of the terrible twos, threatening threes, and fearsome fours dressed their giddy offspring in football jerseys, strapping helmets on their vulnerable heads for protection from deliberate collisions. Chris was number forty-four.

An older student's family served as Chris's stand-in grandparents while Jane worked. During a trip to the mall one day, they couldn't resist having an instant photo made of him. He was grumpy and uncooperative, so they settled for less than the usual smiling pose. Rather, the camera captured a candid shot of Chris with a large tear welled in his eye. Rick and Jane laughed when they saw it. Pleased with its natural quality, they had it blown into a life-sized poster.

Those Kirchoffs certainly enjoyed their child! They walked in the rain together, and hoed their section of a campus garden together. Love was the name of the game for our gentle neighbors. The only fear that passed between them was how unbearable it would be to have a child who, through some quirk of fate, lost his ability to function. They had known of some cases like that, and felt they would not have strength to cope with such a situation. They had nothing to worry about. Chris was so beautifully whole and bright, and cautious about buckling up whenever the car was in motion. Still, his parents made sure his helmet was on before crashing tricycles with his playmates.

I wasn't as careful with my four charges. But then, there were so many ways the Kirchoffs tended each other. On their wall hung a little saying, "Be of love a little more careful than of any other thing." They lived it.

Two years into campus life, a heart wrenching scene unfolded. Shellie's best friend, Jenny, had to move away. Her daddy had graduated and taken a pastoral appointment in North Carolina. As they waved their last good-byes, a profound sadness engulfed our little girl. Chris was the cute small-fry next door, but Jenny did "girl things" with Shellie. They often strolled down to the pond and danced on the concrete bench overlooking it while singing "Que sera, sera?"

Imagining what they would be when they grew into ladies, they spun dreams together and giggled their way back home. With Jenny gone, nothing seemed right. The long summer lay ahead like an endless hurt.

Sensing the depth of grief our child felt, I made a hasty trip to town. Shellie had shown signs of an artistic bent early on, so I scooped up a load of crayons and paints, art paper and construction paper, and presented her with an option for her loneliness.

It seemed like a good plan, but she still moped. I was working around the kitchen one day when I knocked an orange glass mug off the table beside her. It broke to smithereens. I grabbed the broom and dustpan, swept it up and tossed it in the trash, then went about my business unaware of the miracle taking place in my kitchen.

Shellie had gone to the trash container and carefully retrieved the broken pieces. She then spread them out in the form of a flower and drew a nice, green stem beneath. A couple of graceful leaves hugged the stem, making it a whole thing of beauty. She proudly showed me her flower the next time I passed the table. The summer had taken a turn for the better.

That was the beginning of an answer to her sing-song question: "What will I be?" And the beginning of a year without Jenny; but the broken pieces of a young heart had begun to take the shape of a pretty flower. Flowers bloom when it's time. She would, too.

Our last year on campus delivered multiple sicknesses and hospitalizations for our family. Shellie's two bouts with Primary Peritonitis sandwiched her little brother's hospitalization with pneumonia. Shellie's surgery had been the same week he was admitted. Their rooms were down the hall from each other, which made visitation easier. By week's end we had worn ourselves to a frazzle running to and fro.

One morning after getting the children home I awoke with a horrid case of muscular flu. Feeling absolutely miserable, far from family support, I asked Dick to have Jane look in on me. I was sure I'd die while he was in class, and it seemed only fair that someone should know it. Jane was elected.

We left the utility room doors open, enabling her to peek in from time to time to see if I was still "with it." Surprisingly, I survived. My appreciation for her care was so great that I determined to be available if she ever needed me. With seminary days nearing an end, we would go our separate ways. Still, we would remain friends; and friends pay no heed to distance.

Recovery from the flu was far speedier than recovery from years of emotional turmoil. I continued making good, though slow, progress in counseling. Then an amazing phenomenon introduced itself during those remarkable days when the fog of depression began to lift – ever so slowly.

A most exciting adventure unfolded in my dreams. Only during the dark of night, when daytime defenses rested, did I get my emotional bearings. When my guard was down, and the campus population slept, a panorama of dreams provided a compass to lead me through the fog. Dreams allowed me to touch the reality of things that were happening deep inside, where light of understanding hadn't yet penetrated.

Until those nightly journeys occurred, dreams seemed to exist as a mere psychological release mechanism. In time, I came to believe that the Paraclete, the One Who comes alongside, guides, protects, and teaches, led me through that part of my fogged-in life. With thanksgiving, I recall the wondrous ways of God with me via "mind movies."

The Lord knew I was still unable to embrace spiritual jargon, even though my husband was studying to become a pastor. I had clung to high ideals for the church, but nobody measured up. Still bitter about the absence of saints during my earlier years of crisis, and not being ready for religiosity, God spoke to me in ways I could accept: dreams.

The dreams were explicit, vivid, meaningful, informative, colorful, and packed with feeling. They poured through me night after night. Their color and intensity amazed me. Some had such exciting impact I had to share them with Dr. B., whether late at night or early in the morning. I drove to his home late one night to spill out a particularly important dream in great detail. He listened intently, like an adult listens to a child who has discovered something of consequence for the first time.

Several years before entering therapy, I often dreamed of ominous, heavy, black, cloud-drenched seas. The clouds always boiled toward me. Indescribable dread welled up inside as overwhelming darkness, churning breakers, and swirling clouds swept toward me. Gradually, during therapy, the seascape changed. One unforgettable night, I found myself on an exotic slope, climbing a steep, sandy hill. It was slow going, requiring much effort. But once I reached the top I beheld the most beautiful, lushly blue, peaceful lagoon my mind could imagine. It took my breath away.

When I awoke, I knew the "climb" was worth it all, and that one day I could behold a place of inner peace. In the meantime, I trusted that such a place awaited me. Two years later, while vacationing near Lake Michigan, the dream became reality.

We had pulled into a secluded, unoccupied lake lot to walk up an inviting sand dune. Trudging up the steep hill reminded me of the labor involved in leaving low emotional ground to ascend to a better vantage point. Finally, my straining muscles carried me to the top of the dune hill, where the view stunned me. It literally took my breath away, as in my dream. There, as far as eye could see, sprawled an endless expanse of brilliant blue water, calm and glorious!

It was a moment of promise that God was with me. With the promise came a challenge to persevere whenever emotional fog threatened to close in on me, for recovery wasn't yet complete. Other dreams verified what was happening within as I moved from my old self (house) to the new.

MY HOUSE

I was changing.
My dreams told me so.
Vividly.
They took me back,
In night flights
Of the unconscious,
To my childhood home;
The house Dad built.
In the beginning,
The house was in shambles.
It appeared irreparable,
As if it had been
The prime target
In a war zone.
I viewed it with dismay.
My next dream revealed
People who were attempting
To clear away the mess.
I admired them for trying,
But it all seemed
Too impossible…
So much to do;
Where to begin?

They began at the beginning,
With simple
Little things,
Which had to be moved
In order to reach
The big things.
Each time I passed
The house (my unconscious),
There was some kind of
Interesting activity there.
In one dream,
I was amazed to find
A new foundation
Had been laid;
New under-girding,
Strong and solid.
Another time,
The second floor appeared
All new, yet unfinished.
When it did look finished,
It was like before the war –
Neat and clean.
Bright, colorful curtains
Hung in the windows.
The house was really looking
Most presentable
And very attractive.
One night,
I returned to find
A new person
In my house.
I felt a twinge of resentment,
Thinking,
She has no business there!
When I woke up I thought,
"It's okay.
I like the new occupant.
I really don't need to go back there
Anymore."

When I began therapy, old snake dreams, which jolted me awake in younger years, disappeared. Also, the lurking man, my enemy, vanished. Deliberately setting out to change behavior makes the snakes of life flee!

Dr. B. had saved my fleshly life through his personal caring and professional skill. I was deeply moved by his life, for he had not treated me as a patient; he had responded to me as a person. A person of worth. He helped me identify and appreciate my unique personality to the degree that I felt thankful to be me – quite a contrast to the previous thirty years.

Because of my profound gratitude and genuine love for the doctor, I found it hard to break loose of my excessive dependency, professionally termed "transference." That is an inadequate, icy word for what had become a rich, warm relationship. But the time had come to quit memorializing those golden moments of discovery and breakthrough in counseling. I had to say good-bye to the past, hello to the future; good-bye to a doctor, hello to a friend.

BUTTERFLY

You fluttered by
In the night of life
When there were no pretties.
Unable to see in the dark,
I sensed the rhythm
Of your wings and listened…
Then came a ray of light.
I saw your brilliance
Fill the midnight sky.
Like any color-deprived soul would do,
I ooh-ed and ahh-ed
And tried to capture you.
It's hard to hold a butterfly,
So I put you under glass,
Hoping I could keep the past.
The night of life is gone.
Here, now, is the glorious dawn.
Upon the sun's rising,
I hold you to the sky
And let you fly
Away,

SEVEN

Bumps and Bruises

May, 1970, Dick graduated at the top of his seminary class. Although it had been a turbulent, spectacular wedge of life, we were itching to move into a real house. Our dinky apartment held many good memories, but the children had grown three years' worth. They needed room to be normal, room for privacy, room for junk.

The usual last minute frenzy of pastoral appointments for graduating students left us on pins and needles until just before graduation. Calls with offers of positions kept campus phones ringing and the student grapevine active. Seniors daily compared notes on where they'd be going, salary packages, parsonage set-ups, and sizes of congregations.

We had planned to return to Michigan. That was home. The first call we received we accepted; partly because it was an attractive package, and partly because there wasn't much left from which to choose. We were given one day to give our answer.

The offer was of special interest because the church was in our home town, where my parents lived. Not only that, it was the church we had rented for our wedding reception 15 years earlier. The children would have the opportunity to know their grandparents better, so we said "yes."

From a practical point of view, the parsonage was perfect. It was a beautiful, spacious, fairly new two story home right near a school. Being located in an older neighborhood, the house stuck out like a sore thumb. We didn't know then that our house, with oodles of big rooms and walk-in closets, would be such a bone of contention with neighbors and parishioners alike. We loved the space, including room for a real bed for each of us. It more than made up for three years of being cramped, and looked like a grand place to begin our ministry. But looks are deceiving.

Within a very short period of time, we found that our lovely new house was a source of contention to those living nearby, including a few of our parishioners. The children came to me with comments their play-mates' parents had made about having to foot the bill for us to live there. Remarks continually filtered through about our house being tax-free, and not really ours. Such remarks were obviously hatched by resentful adults. Our house felt like anything but home, sweet home.

If upstairs lights were left on, we got phone calls about it. If the boys' ball rolled into someone's yard, police were called. One snowy day, two of our boys moved a neighbor's snowman to a different yard. The police came to take an official report. That night's newspaper edition told the story: "Frosty the Snowman Stolen!"

The pressure of living in a fishbowl didn't bode well for our older sons. Like many preacher's kids, they went the extra mile to prove they were free spirits. Their "free spirits" threw one of our church member neighbors into a tizzy one ordinary day. I answered the kitchen phone, which allowed me a clear view to the caller's house. A tirade of angry scolding came scooting across our yards via a telephone wire.

It seemed that Steve and Jim had climbed our steep second story roof without my knowledge, but in full view of the yelping man. "Your kids are on the roof! I helped pay for that roof, and they're damaging it!" I had a different concern: Would they get off it alive, or would I find them splattered all over the church-paid-for sidewalk? The boys survived their descent from the precarious perch, but I developed some giant resent-ments before they crawled inside.

Granted, my crew didn't approach perfection, but people would-n't let us just be us. They wanted a faultless family, which we weren't. Old anxieties returned, plus a growing disappointment in God's people. Didn't anybody know how to be kind? Just kind? Parsonage life wasn't very pleasant. And the preacher's wife role didn't fit well at all. It made me miserable. No one seemed interested in who I was - just who I was supposed to be.

After awhile, I withdrew from the role altogether, going to serv-ices only when it suited me. Women's groups were avoided, and I opted out of serving at dinners. I always cut the pie wrong, or put things in the wrong place anyway. Being invisible at such functions didn't set well with persons who felt they had hired *two* parsonage hands, so resentments smoldered on both sides. Something was missing, in spite of all my achievements. I was able to cope, but coping wasn't enough. I again entered into counseling for a brief time.

We scraped through two years of an impotent ministry in my home town and made plans to return to Delaware, Ohio. Dick signed up for two years of chaplain training residency, teaching part time at the seminary he had attended. The arrangement would give us some relief from parsonage pressures. Since some of our children proved their individuality by going overboard in the direction of mischief, being out of the limelight might help.

We decided to move back into their former school district so they could continue friendships that were made during seminary years. The rural setting seemed an ideal growing up place. After unsuccessful house hunting, we bought a large mobile home. We would live in a mobile home village just a half-mile from the school. Living in Michigan during the planning phase necessitated long distance business arrangements. We bought the mobile home via phone and mail, and were assured that all was in order. It would be set up in time for our arrival date.

I was so eager to leave the miserable failure behind that the children and I, and Millie, our cat, left in the wee hours of Sunday morning. Dick remained behind for one last sermon. He would drive the loaded U-Haul to Ohio that afternoon.

We had an uneventful trip, in spite of our frantic cat. Seven hours after hitting the road, I got a key to our new home from its pre-arranged hiding place. The home looked like paradise, though much smaller than the parsonage we left behind.

The mobile home sales lot was situated directly in front of the residential park, so we assumed it was a combined business. It was closed when we arrived. Everything seemed to be in order. With no furniture there yet, the children and I drove around, then sat on the carpet and waited until Dick came.

Just as evening fell, the truck came rolling in. A car followed closely behind. Dick braked, opened the door, and stepped down. The car behind screeched to a stop, and a man lurched out in front of him with a barrage of cursing, asking what we thought we were doing. My husband's jaw dropped in disbelief. He informed him that we *were* moving into our new home. We were then told in no uncertain terms that we could not move in. He was the park manager, and no such arrangements had been made.

"Don't bother unloading!" he snapped. Until we signed papers and had been approved by management (in Cincinnati) we were not welcome.

I stood in the street crying. The children were scared. Dick responded that we were moving in, and arrangements had been made. He lowered the truck ramp and started handing out household items. As the man jerked his car door open to leave, he snarled a warning; "Be in my office at one o'clock tomorrow…or else!"

Dick had been hired to start a temporary summer job with the highway department at eight o'clock the next morning. I would have to face the man alone since my husband couldn't risk losing his job.

I appeared promptly at one. The man's wife, who served as his secretary, coldly informed me that we couldn't live there; we had one too many kids. I fleetingly wondered which one I was to get rid of, but my funny bone kicked out of gear pronto. She seemed to be getting some sort of pleasure from scaring me. I felt trapped. There, across the pond, sat our newly mortgaged, very large un-mobile mobile home on a lot for which we hadn't been approved, and in a park that didn't allow more than five persons per home. Now what?

She said she'd call the home office in Cincinnati and see what should be done. I waited, tightening like a spring inside, while she negotiated. After a brief conversation, our illegal family of six suddenly changed status. We were acceptable, after all. I signed papers and headed for my next door neighbor to phone the mobile home salesman. In a sputter of tears and barbed words, the events surrounding our arrival landed on his ears. Within minutes, he came to personally apologize for the mix-up. Then I relaxed.

The whole summer lay before us – a summer that would be enjoyable, what with a big park swimming pool right across the way. But the park manager continued to harass us at every opportunity. Very often I could hear him cursing or yelling, usually both, at our children, or someone else's. He didn't seem capable of speaking matter-of-factly, let alone kindly. I detested living in what felt more like a prison camp than a residential community.

As the end of summer approached, my daughter and I took advantage of the pool. She was 12. I stretched out on a lawn chair, watching Shellie play on the concrete apron. She lifted a metal lid of some kind and put her shoe in it. I told her not to play there, so she retrieved the shoe and walked toward me. Just then, in earshot of an entire pool population, the booming voice of our disgruntled park manager cut through the air from behind me. "Get the ____ out of there! And don't touch it again!"

He had intimidated me so badly since the night we moved in, I could hardly believe what happened next. I lurched from the chair, just as he had lurched from his car that first night, walked toward him, and looked straight in his threatening eyes. "That wasn't necessary. Now you quit bothering us once and for all!" My anger boiled over like a kettle of water left on "high" too long.

I didn't appreciate or realize the significance of standing up to him until that night, when the old lurking man/enemy dream reappeared, this time with a new twist.

AUGUST 26, 1972

All of my life I've had dreams of being chased, hunted, or pursued, often in a war situation. These were very frustrating dreams because I was so frightened, and the weapons I had never worked. They were either empty or faulty or turned out to be toys with no power whatsoever. Often I escaped by hiding or running. I never won in any previous dream.

From the instant this dream began, I was unafraid. I felt a confident strength – a quiet, sure kind of strength – that I would win. There was no doubt about it. The task was to finish completely, regardless of how long it would take.

The enemy and I were alone. He had the form of a man. His face was unimportant and unrecognizable. He was very tall and lean, dressed in military khakis. He never uttered a sound. Neither did I.

From the start, I had a grip on him. I caught him by the throat the same instant I faced him and saw his eyes. He struggled and struggled, but I never loosened my grip, nor did there seem a possibility that I would. He kept twisting to get free, but I was choking him to death. I knew all his twisting couldn't stop that. The thought that I was actually murderous occurred to me in the dream. It seemed incredible, yet necessary, that I would deliberately and cold-bloodedly squeeze the life out of him. I remember the element of surprise I felt with that realization.

There was a brief time when the enemy's allies intruded. Enemy and I were in secrecy, as in an underground war story, and he was wiggling. I was afraid they would see him, so I lifted him over the back of the sofa with one hand, and casually motioned the soldiers in another direction with the other. Meantime, I kept my grip and choked him with one hand.

I was alone with him again, so I dragged him out in front of me. He was not going to die easily. He twisted and writhed like the snakes in former dreams; twisting and writhing, writhing and twisting. I decided to place him in a large plastic bag. It was black and very long, because he was so tall. I tied the bag and watched him wiggle some more. He did not want to die.

The dream was very long, but no effort seemed to be expended. Finally, after watching him squirm for a long period of time, he died. I was sure of it. It surprised me to see that when he died, he had become very small. The bag was small enough to be held in one hand, and it was weightless.

What was the significance of this dream? It was the point in my life when I faced fear - the thing that had kept me running and intimidated in a million little ways all of my life. Fear was the biggest deciding factor until then. It kept me from walking down streets. It kept me from entering into conversations. It kept me bound. I had done a better job of managing and coping since therapy, but fear still lingered in the little corners of my being.

Living in the park with a hostile, harassing manager had caused those trapped, fearful feelings to surface again. Facing up to him instead of letting him scare me that summer day in '72 broke the hold of fear on me. I faced the enemy. In doing so, I discovered that the real enemy lived within, and found that the gigantic thing controlling me for so long didn't have any weight at all. What a revelation! Fear didn't weigh *anything* when it was faced. I felt "high" for five weeks after that dream. I was free.

Dr. B. and his family had become dear friends during our time at seminary. They moved to Germany for a sabbatical leave a few days before we moved into our mobile home. Their year away seemed endless. The active correspondence we had maintained since leaving Ohio took a leap across the ocean, making our friendship even closer and more special. They had stuck with us through thick and thin. I wanted to be the same kind of friend to them…true blue.

DICK AND ELLEN

A year without a friend
Can be a lifetime.
It seemed that way.
The best times
Were 'way out there

Somewhere.
It seemed as if
We'd never know
Each other's touch again
And yet we knew,
In the scheme of things –
In time,
We would.
We dreamed a lot
Of days ahead;
Homecoming,
Sharing good times.
We played little tricks
With our loneliness
Like –
"Oh, a year isn't very long."
Or,
"There really are a lot of
Interesting things to do
While waiting."
Ha. Ha. Ha.
Such hollow pastimes!
A year *was* a long time
Without them.
We coped.
That's all.
Found how very precious
Some folks are
And felt so blessed
To have friends like them.
June. July. August. September.
October. November. December.
January. February. March.
April. May. June.
The year somehow
Pulled itself
Through the knothole.
Then came the glad reunion day
When their planc glided,
With all grace,

To the ground below,
And taxied to our waiting place.
I melted,
Along with the empty year,
Gulped in the morning air,
Skipped a heartbeat,
And thrilled to
The moment's treasure.
The world spun on its axis
Once more
As we took them home
And picked up
Friendship's lovely reins.

Dick and Ellen loved me as I was, knowing I had healed from many emotional bumps and bruises while fighting my way to life. Spiritual bumps and bruises, some inflicted, some invited, were harder to overcome. Resisting anything that smacked of religion, I decided I was through with God. But He wasn't through with me. His golden thread of grace kept slipping around me in this way and that. Knowing I wouldn't settle for fool's gold (religiosity), He gave me the Real Thing; that for which I had yearned in wordless ways since the day I first set my thoughts on Him in the snow bank.

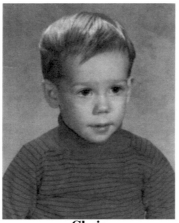

Chris

EIGHT

Christmas, 1973

Our friends, the Kirchoffs, had received a pastoral appointment in Paducah, Kentucky upon graduation. Christmas Eve, 1973, they packed their car with luggage and gifts to spend the holiday week with Jane's family in Selmer, Tennessee. The trip took about three hours. Chris, six years old by then, and adopted three year old daughter Julie, squirmed all the way in anticipation of the great gift-giving event.

Christmas unfolded right on schedule. It was nice to be home again where the children could relish in their grand-parent's affection and attention. Julie's eyes twinkled like the lights on the tree as she scanned her abundance of presents. Chris tingled all the way down to his toes when he unwrapped his very own basketball; the gift he had most wanted every since he astonished himself (and his dad) by sinking a ball through the hoop. He could hardly wait to get back home and try it, as soon as his dad put up a backboard and net. Then he would dazzle them both!

Christmas day turned inside out, reluctantly giving way to December twenty-sixth. That morning, in Delaware, I fought the losing battle of customer vs. store policy. A gift didn't fit. Things were picked over. Nothing in sight was worth taking home, but the rules said "No

Refund." Fuming, I left without gift or refund, noting how quickly the Christmas spirit had departed store personnel, and me.

I moved across the street to open a bank account for my son, then slipped through slush on up the street to buy new license plates for the car. There, I acquired another knot in my stomach as the clerk's hostility for her job found a target in those of us needing service. I felt wrung out by the time she had finished her rat-a-tat-tat treatment of people's inquiries, and returned home feeling very sorry for myself. It was one of those days a person prefers to back up and start over.

That same morning, in Selmer, Jane spent some time playing with Julie and her new toys while Chris and his cousin, Mike, got bundled up for a trip to the store with their grandpa. They had some Christmas money to spend. Out the door they scurried, racing each other to the car. Rick sank down in the bathtub for a good post-Christmas soak. His hair frothy with shampoo, he leaned back for some warm, luxurious relaxation. It felt so good to do nothing, just bask in the joy of Christmas. When the phone rang it jerked Christmas joy from memory, creating a day they, too, would prefer to back up and start over.

December 27th, while working at the kitchen sink, still snorting about the frustrating day before, our phone rang. My daughter answered it. "It's Mrs. Kirchoff." It was rare for Jane to call, but to call mid-day when rates were highest...? I greeted her with a too-quick and cheery, "Hi! How are you?" An intuitive knowledge that something was wrong hadn't caught up with my words in time.

With her soft voice in tight control, she said, "Hi. There's been an accident." In that split second spinning of the brain, I thought she must be talking about Rick. By the time I formulated the thought, she added, "Chris is hurt."

Jane went on to say that her father, nephew, and son had been thrown through the windshield when their car collided head-on with a truck. The accident had happened close to their home, so the boys never made it to the store for their shopping spree. None of the three were buckled up. All were in critical condition in the Intensive Care Unit, but Chris was the most severely injured. With massive internal and head injuries, no one was sure he would survive.

Jane's voice was taut, distant. She was hanging on for dear life – Chris's. After hanging up, my children and I cried for our little friend.

In my reflective moments, my mind replayed the day I read Dick's letter about breaking our romance. Unable to move for several hours from the shock of his "new girl" news, it felt like dead weight.

Numbing. A lonely grief. Not so with the news of Chris. Taking the burden of it in tow, I moved swiftly toward others who knew them, as Jane had requested; the seminary dean, former classmates and professors, congregations Rick had served as a student pastor.

Ensuing days and weeks spilled over with thoughts of Rick, Jane, and Chris. The phone became a source of anxiety and anticipation as I feared its message, yet waited for word. Sometimes I called the hospital waiting room, not wanting to be a nuisance, but too tense to passively wait. I longed to be there with them. That being impossible, they were entrusted to the care of those who were there, and we continued to wait.

The Dean of the seminary had formerly pastored churches in Tennessee, maintaining an affiliation with the church conference leadership in that area. He immediately contacted people who might lend assistance to the family. We faithfully relayed information back and forth as it became available.

Through the Dean I learned of a stream of ministers who frequented the hospital, offering support and comfort. Upon leaving, they pressed fistfuls of money in Rick's hand to relieve financial pressures. It was a long way from home, and looked like an indeterminate stay. Hell had become a very real place; a place they had entered involuntarily for an unknown length of time. With winter's icy grip within and without, the need for God grew.

ECLIPSE

The day becomes
Mysteriously hung
'Tween Now and Then.
The sun (future)
Seems harmless enough,
But to look direct
Might blind their human eyes.
Therefore,
They behold the murky mist of Now,
And hope for a clear, safe dawn
Tomorrow.

When living next door to Chris at the seminary, he was just the neighbor boy. Though my four children paid attention to him, there was no particular closeness between Chris and me. Following the accident, however, I developed an intensely intimate relationship of spirit with him. His suffering was suddenly mine to explore and experience. I knew deep down that I was engaged in an all-out encounter with God.

I felt overwhelmed in the beginning, just as everyone else did. Useless. There seemed to be so little a person could do. The disadvantage of 500 miles between didn't help matters. Yet, helplessness proved to be the point of power. Specifically, it provoked me to deal with God; or was it the other way around?

As a teen, I was a conscientious Christian, and held to the moralistic traditions of my church. Though new at the task of living a believer's life when I met Dick, I took it seriously. With time, it grew increasingly difficult to live up to the high expectations of myself and others. The inconsistencies of church people, their seeming absence during my neediness in young adulthood, plus my own failures, left me disillusioned. I was too idealistic to last long, the church too realistic with its population of gossips and critics to keep me.

I abandoned my goal of being a "good" Christian, and settled for being a good person. That was a major error. There is no goodness apart from God. But, like crooning Frank Sinatra, I had to do things *my* way.

Church attendance continued, minus passion. Being married to a minister I eventually acquiesced, assuming a role defined by some other generation. It didn't fit me, or vice-versa. How could it? I didn't yet know me, or the God who made me - not to the degree needed for *real* identity. Most of my marriage, I was out of tune with the Gospel, and in rebellion against the church. The words "Chris is hurt" woke a dormant root of desire to know God, so I entered into a search for the mysteries of faith.

Having never understood the meaning of prayer, or why it was necessary, a great resistance to it had developed over the years. By the time I had a need to pray for Chris, I felt like a stranger trespassing on someone else's property.

SIGHTSEER

I look upon a place that's
New to me
And try to soak in

All its history.
I wonder at its age,
Its story,
And yearn to know its depth.
But in its silence,
It shouts
That it cannot be mine,
Nor can I belong to it,
Because we have not
Shared the past.
And I,
Trespassing –
And on the holy ground of age,
Must go home
Where I belong.

I had nowhere to go, though. Not knowing where I belonged, and without a faith-home, I had to build one. In spite of my discomfort, I began to pray for my friends. I asked for healing for Chris. That's a lot to ask of a Stranger! I asked with hope, which then passed for faith.

Tucked inside that hopeful asking was a mountain of doubt. I really didn't know what I was doing, or why God should listen to me, but I asked anyway. Hoping he wouldn't hold up the gift of healing for a six year old boy because of my rusty faith, I simply asked for Chris to get well, and strength for Rick and Jane if he didn't. Now there was a quandary for God! But it was a starting point, and God always honors starting points.

I tried to examine as honestly as I could why prayer irked me. Apart from the obvious fact that I was not living close to God, I felt as if prayer was too often a cop-out. People, it appeared, prayed in order to "pass the buck", not wanting to use their common sense in a situation. Or, perhaps people prayed to earn points with God by using clever, impressive arrangements of verbiage.

Recalling people who prayed words for me, but never put feet to them when I was so desperate, provided an excuse – briefly. Leafing through memory pages of the past, I was forced to admit that a few folks had successfully linked their prayers with deeds. Regardless, the suggestion "Let's pray about it" was a red flag for me.

A big flag went up my spiritual spine (or lack of) when a group tried to decide what time to schedule a film for the following Sunday. We had gotten through the nuts and bolts of time conflicts fairly well. The loose ends were coming together nicely when someone said "Let's pray about it." I was furious, for as soon as the prayer ascended we returned to the task of nailing down a time! What help was it? Surely God expected us to assume responsibility for such basics.

I thought He would be better off answering prayers going up on behalf of hurting people in this world. My focus was Chris, of course. And if He could fiddle around granting the wishes of a lady who fretted about a film time, why couldn't He answer the prayers of two broken-hearted parents who grieved over their son, who was more dead than alive? It didn't make sense. Neither did the intensity of my anger. A battle was raging that magnified many insignificant things into major issues. The war was on!

In my ignorance, I questioned God's ability to handle *anything* appropriately. He seemed absent. I grew increasingly uneasy asking Him for help. No matter how, why, when, or where I asked, I felt manipulative – like I had in therapy 'way back when the lid blew off. I couldn't free myself of the disgusting feeling that, in asking, I opened myself up to rejection. Demanding answers, I felt like He would slap me down. Begging, I felt cheap.

Suddenly, I was trying to get home for lunch, wondering which tactic would best work on the kid with the snowballs. Equating God with a bully, He and I couldn't get eyeball to eyeball long enough to work out the kinks. I interpreted His absence as being punitive, blind to my monumental lack of knowledge concerning Him and His ways.

People commented on Chris's progress (a blink of the eye or twitch of a muscle) as being God's doing. As far as I was concerned, Rick and Jane were doing the doing - twenty four hours a day of it - to the exclusion of their own needs and pleasures. I failed to see God at work in the situation. My initial baby grudge had escalated into a full-fledged monster.

I had agenda wherever I went. It seemed best to stay away from the Sunday morning Bible study, what with my persistent agitation. In spite of my struggle, I didn't want to be the devil's advocate all the time, possibly scorching someone's newly sprouted faith with my heavy artillery of doubt. There had to be an answer somewhere, but I was always in the wrong place at the wrong time with the wrong questions. Or was I?

Soon after the accident, I experienced two vivid dreams regarding Chris. The first one had a terrific impact, shaking me to the core. It both perplexed and exhilarated me. In the dream four words came to me: "It's a dancing seal." That's all. There was no visual image or dream story; just words which registered deep inside and were gently, firmly branded there as by some searing, painless fire. The words were powerfully reassuring, yet their meaning escaped me.

I searched for a description of seals with no satisfaction. I ended up making the observation that seals are a delight to their audience and, though limited by their physical characteristics, are able to perform feats of grace for less graceful bystanders. Did that mean Chris, and those of us nearby? A dancing seal, then, must mean a creature with extraordinary skills. I entertained that speculation for awhile, knowing it was not the full answer.

Exactly a week later I had a second dream. It was clearly related to the first, as if an explanation. Again, four powerful words emanated from my innermost being. They said, "It's in the Scriptures." They, too, were burned deep within and remain a part of me to this day. A search of a Bible concordance shed no light on the subject, so I filed the words away in my mind and spirit. The import of them, however, continues to convince me that Chris's life purpose is wrapped up in them, as is mine.

My little friend's seventh birthday was coming up Valentine's Day. Being engrossed with the symbol of the seal, I decided to "act out" the acceptance of the mysterious dream message by crocheting an afghan. On the reverse side, I would apply a seal made of plain material. This was an ambitious undertaking considering the fact that I only knew how to crochet hot pads. Aunt Bea had taught me how when I was a little girl. I mused that if she was looking down from above, she might wince at how little I had learned. Somehow, my squares didn't "square" like hers did.

Dozens of mini-hot pads piled up beside me as I spent hours and days working my sense of helplessness into thousands of loops. With the completion of each irregular, unattractive square, I hoped for release from the awful agony of merely waiting, while a dear little life tried to "make it" some 500 miles away. Any self-respecting person would have been embarrassed to send such a thing, but it arrived in time for Chris's birthday. I felt a little better having expressed my faith in the dream message, and drew yet closer to Chris during those hours of concentration.

The dreams continued. Often they flashed scenes of Chris speaking for the first time as my unconscious leaked out its deep desire for that.

I asked to be called night or day – the minute he woke up – assuming that he would indeed wake up and be okay, and the ordeal would be over. After several months of waiting, I knew it wouldn't be that easy – and relaxed my vigil by the phone.

WAITIN'
Ain't that phone ever gonna ring?
Aint' that boy ever gonna sing?
Ain't that letter ever gonna bring
Good news?

NINE

Easter, 1974

I talked about Chris with a minister friend on Good Friday. I had utterly failed the test for understanding trials and tribulations. After airing my spiritual confusion and disappointment, he helped me focus the enormity of my anger toward God. Anger was something I disguised as "concern." "Concern" felt better. After admitting the disagreeable angry part of myself, my friend set me on a new train of thought. I hadn't gotten the answers I'd hoped for, but I came away with resolve to dig deeper.

The minister suggested that most people think of a productive life (in the case of a young boy) as being a child who can play ball, run bases, ride bikes, etc. His observation was that most boys who run bases and catch fly balls are content to have fun. But chances are not too many of them change anybody's life by doing so. He was not saying it was wrong, or even inferior, to simply be "typical", nor was there glory in agony. He simply threw out a challenge to look beyond Chris's limitation and see what he was achieving *in* it.

So I looked very carefully at his seven year old life and came to an unexpected conclusion: Chris was doing far more than is generally expected of a child. Not that it was a consolation to his parents or any of us that he could not move or talk, but I could see a ray of truth pushing its way through the cloud of suffering.

Everyone involved had been hoping for an Easter miracle. A hospital chaplain put us in touch with a lady whom some doctors called on in unusual cases like Chris's. She had a reputation for having the capacity to enter into the unconscious of another person and give doctors "readings" on patients' thoughts and physical problems. It's not with pride that I share this period of spiritual ignorance and sin against a holy God, but with hope that persons feeling similar helplessness will not resort to the same useless measures.

Only the Divine Helper must be consulted and trusted. At the time, however, I placed some trust in the woman. She seemed genuinely interested in Chris and his family. After several conversations with her, I became convinced that Chris would be talking by Easter morning. It seemed like the perfect time for God to reveal His resurrection power; to show the world, me included, how it could be done. I had it all figured out: Chris would rise to health on Easter morning, and all would be well. It didn't happen that way.

Chris was not only unable to talk or play ball like other boys, he could not control any part of his body. His head had to be propped in place, and his arms pried away from his bony chest in order to be exercised or washed. His eyes couldn't focus so that, although he leaned toward sound, no one was sure he could see or recognize those around him. His voice had been silent since December twenty-sixth. How much he comprehended, no one knew. It struck me with the weight of lead that a newborn baby had more coordination than Chris. In fact, newborn abilities were like Olympic skills in comparison. It hurt to think how far he had to go just to catch up with a brand new baby.

When Easter came and went without a resurrection of Chris, I lost confidence in the lady psychic and returned to the question at hand: "What is the goal for a human life?" I wrestled with the question unceasingly, using the brief conversation with my minister friend as a starting point.

Before long I made the startling discovery that Chris, in his unconsciousness, had already achieved the highest of missions: he had caused people around him to deal with God, and journey to the Cross. He was having a profound impact *in his helplessness* that strong boys running bases were not.

Chris was not injured *so that* I might encounter the real issues of life. But, *in response* to his injuries, I indeed encountered issues of utmost importance. Chris was not broken *so that* I might appreciate my children's wholeness, yet *in response* to his brokenness, I became keenly aware of their taken-for-granted health. Chris was not *placed in jeopardy* to teach anyone anything, but *in response* to his tragedy, many people learned valuable lessons about the broader nature of love and worthwhile priorities. Life came into clearer focus for those of us who were foolishly absorbed in such non-essentials as what to buy next or what to busy ourselves with in order to break the boredom of living

So Christopher Paul had something going for him. I thought, "Oh, Lord, this boy – in his brokenness – has already accomplished what I, in my healthy lifetime, have not." He drew out the best in people, not by choice, but by circumstance. With a bite of the lip I admitted that, with full capabilities, I had not done that much in thirty-six years.

Though perceived as being whole, I had been broken in many ways: emotionally, spiritually, relationally. The dream of my heart had been shattered along life's way, leading me to abort the idea I could succeed in things that count. Yes, there was personal brokenness to be reckoned with. Chris enabled me to admit it.

Many persons pooled similar brokennesses to help Chris, investing time, energy, money, prayer, support of every imaginable kind to aid in his recovery. Selfishness gave way to selflessness as narrow horizons expanded to include the care of a little boy. As he received all that was given, I learned yet more about the blessing of *receiving*. Chris was teaching magnificent lessons unaware.

The little guy was physically vulnerable; totally at the mercy of those around him. My mind began to process what it meant to be vulnerable, likening his receptivity to physical care to my need for equal openness spiritually. If his broken body had one outstanding lesson worth my learning, it was this: total receptivity. Just as God rushed in to provide Chris and his family with what was needed in the way of persons, finances, and strength, so He desired to do the same with me – in the spirit – if I could just become vulnerable enough to receive from His hand.

What freedom Chris had in his bondage! What bondage I felt in my freedom, for my bindings were more complex. The self-sufficient body they wrapped, and the false notion that I could handle life in my own strength, tied me up in knots. Because I had learned to cope emotionally, I thought that was all I needed. But there remained a big, empty space needing to be filled. Chris magnified that need, moving me to face my own peculiar handicaps. In doing so, I realized that being "normal" was not necessarily a one-way ticket to paradise. And a "normal" body had little to do with a normal or healthy heart. My body worked. My spiritual heart didn't.

I looked at the state of affairs with Chris and concluded that when this child, without the use of a good deal of his nerves, muscles, and cells, exercised for ten hours a day – just to crawl ten feet of rug space – he had produced a hundred per cent. That was achievement! That was using all he had the best he could. That was pulling out all the stops and going whole hog without much to work with, not to gain some national recognition or gold medal award, but to hear a squeal of joy from his fans, and earn a grin for himself.

Was there more to be desired in me, the "normal" person who had all my health intact? How many times had I wandered aimlessly about, wondering how to fill a day? The wasteland lay in me, who ignored my potential so much of the time. I had indulged in the subtle violence of various prejudices, as well as relational and spiritual neglect all too often.

While deepening my relationship with a seven year old boy, I inched closer to an ageless God. Still not liking His style, and not yet submitted to all I had learned through Chris, I continued to hammer out a faith, blow by blow, with the One Who created this awful, lovely universe. Despite my arrogance and rebellion, God "took me on" and initiated further teaching such as I had not bargained for. He knew it was time for me to move beyond the realm of the psyche and into the realm of the Spirit.

LAZARUS AND CHRIS AND ME

Oh, Laz'rus,
He came out of the tomb
At the mighty shout of the Lord;
Couldn't wait to breathe in
God's clean air,
'Cause he had been so very dead.
What a shock he must've had
To find that all his health
Could not emerge
'Til someone minded Christ,
Stepped forth,
And unwound all those bindings.
Oh, Chris,
You slept deep down
In the darksome tomb,
Hov'ring nearly dead so long,
'Til Christ said,
"Chris, come forth, My son",
Telling those of us nearby
To rid you of your bindings,
One by one,
That, in the process,
We might lose our own.

TEN

The Way of Love

My first opportunity to visit the Kirchoffs was May of 1974, five months after the accident. A friend offered to drop me off in Paducah on her way to Memphis, so I jumped at the chance to spend a week with my beleaguered friends.

Rick's congregation had helped him convert the parsonage garage into a family room to house Chris's special therapy equipment. As I entered, my gaze fell on Chris, who was lying on a hospital bed. His head was turned toward the television. His eyes reflected the toll of severe physical trauma. He was thin and pale. Wash cloths were wadded up in his small fists to protect his palms from tightly dug-in fingernails which extended from stiff, contorted fingers. As a result of brain damage, his body was extremely rigid. Both legs were drawn up and stiff. There was no evidence of recognition, nor response, when I said, "Hi, Chris. It's Pat."

Unsure of myself, and not really prepared for Chris's appearance, I followed Jane's lead and kept it light. We chattered about food and weight and the trip. I thought, "When your world caves in, maybe you have to control what little you can." She probably thought of me, "When your world hasn't caved in, maybe you don't know what to say." She would have been right.

The family room had been stocked with nursing items, but was colorful and pleasing to the eye. The bed was placed so he could look out the floor-to-ceiling sliding glass door at passing traffic, or the train which whistled and rumbled by their property line twice a day.

Rick and Jane had settled into a routine of care, and had recently begun "patterning" exercises for Chris. This required a battery of volunteers who came in daily to assist with the prescribed therapy. Five ladies came each morning for thirty minute stints, and five more came in the afternoon to repeat the process of moving head, arms, and legs in a particular sequence of movements. First he was sprawled flat on a special table, spread-eagle style. Then each person held a particular limb. The team moved his limbs in order, beginning with the head - left to right, an arm from up to down, the leg up and down, then to the opposite side for the same procedure.

These movements were designed to encourage Chris's brain to send signals for crawling. Once he learned to crawl, he could possibly rise up on all fours, then walk, and finally talk. At this point in his therapy, all movements were done for him by the volunteers. Sessions usually wore Chris out to the point of sleep.

A total of seventy persons a week entered the Kirchoff home. It was an unspeakably large adjustment for Jane, who tended to be timid and quite private. But, being the angels they were, their coming and going was delicately executed and she was none the worse for wear. Jane breathed prayers of gratitude for their faithfulness and concern as she set the coffee pot out for them twice a day.

Chris was spooned baby food, or food the family ground in a blender. He couldn't chew well, making mealtimes lengthy, but they established a workable routine for that portion of the day. Separate responsibilities speeded the process.

I was given what was Chris's former bedroom for my sleeping quarters. The first night lent a strange wakefulness as I considered the room's contents. Chris's bike stood in the corner. Drawings and notes he had printed in school still hung on the walls. One said, in typical first grade scrawl, "I love you, Mom." The closet was filled with boxes of clothes that had rescinded to an onslaught of colorful hospital gowns his grandma had made.

As I reached out to hang my clothes, I spied my dancing seal afghan. It occupied a corner of the closet floor. I didn't blame them. The sense of loss in the room was great as its rightful occupant took up residence in the more functional family therapy room. Was Chris temporarily away? Or permanently? Who could know?

During my stay I was invited to accompany the family to the local Easter Seal Center where Chris received physical therapy two or three times a week. The worker looked closely at Chris and offered kind encouragement to his anxious parents. She drew a tissue across his face, hoping to find some trace of responding muscles or a sign of tear formation as she brushed it around his eyes and nose. She was absolutely ecstatic when Chris's eyes watered and he showed some annoyance with her antics. "Both good signs," she said.

Jane's parents and cousin Mike came to see Chris while I was there. It was an awkward visit, especially for Mike. He had recovered, but hadn't seen Chris since the accident. He talked to Chris, struggling to hide his feelings when the words he spoke died in the air. I could sense him remembering the day he had sat beside Chris in their grandpa's car, looking forward to their trip to the store. Suddenly, he was looking at a cousin who would never be the same, wondering why he was okay and Chris wasn't.

Meanwhile, Rick headed for the garden and chopped weeds to vent his enormous feelings of loss. Tears dripped down his cheeks and dried there in the warm spring sunshine. Inside the house was the man who had driven the car that turned into a curse - the man who hadn't buckled the children in.

CHRIS

Everyone who sees him
Asks questions…
"How are ya, Chris?
Wanna go fishin'?
Can you see me?"
He doesn't answer –
Even with his eyes.

THEIR HOUSE

It's mostly calm,
Has its routine.
But, once in awhile,
The pain leaks out
From its storage place
And feels like too much.

Before I left for home, Jane removed a notebook from the bottom of a desk drawer and handed it to me as if she were giving away her heart.

Very carefully she placed it in my hands and said I could read what no one else had seen: a day-by-day account written during Chris's hospitalization. She hadn't re-read it. She also let me look through old family photo albums, something she hadn't been able to do since Chris had been injured. After reading her story, I knew why reviewing photos was so painful.

ELEVEN

The Way It Was

*Taken from the Journal, with brief
editorial additions by the author.*

We passed the smashed car, but it really didn't sink in how accurately the twisted metal and broken glass recorded the physical condition of our loved ones. Minds were too intent on getting to the hospital. Julie rode in the back seat with her grandma.

Upon arriving at the emergency room we were met by a medical team whose faces wore lines of strain and shadows of weariness. Oblivious to hospital rules, Rick rushed into the treatment area where Chris laid on a stretcher. Before being ushered out he had seen enough of the gravity of the situation to fear for our son's life. He grew weak and headed for a chair.

Mother was hysterical. In spite of the confusion and emotions present in the waiting room, we couldn't help but notice the intern's troubled, bewildered expression as he tried to treat three critical accident victims at once. There registered a very deep appreciation for the doctor's huge task.

Word soon came that Chris must be transferred to Jackson Hospital because of his head injuries. Friends were called to come for Julie. She had been quiet and unsure during the intensity of feeling in the waiting room. She left without protest.

It was agreed that I would ride in the ambulance. Rick followed in the car. For me, the ride was fast and silent. Too silent. It just didn't seem real. I could see Chris as I looked back, but I didn't do that, being afraid of what I might see.

The silence was finally broken by the driver beside me who said, "We've come farther than I thought we would. I didn't think the little one would make it out of the car." I gulped an involuntary gush of air and felt a stab of panic bolt down my spine as I realized the "little one" was my son.

I kept my eyes focused on the road as the siren wailed its warning for cars to get out of the way. The going was rough with extra post-Christmas traffic. I felt faint off and on but breathed deeply per instructions by the driver as we raced toward Jackson.

Rick, following in the little car, tried desperately to keep up with the ambulance. He wept, wiping his eyes often in order to see. Engulfed in waves of fear and disbelief, he called on God for help. Finally, he lost sight of the ambulance and gave up the chase.

At that point, he saw clearly in his mind's eye Chris's head being cradled by strong Hands. Christ's Hands. He prayed, "Cradle him Lord." and resumed the difficult task of maneuvering through traffic. He was not sure Chris would be alive the next time he saw him. The "vision" was temporarily shelved in the subconscious as he hurried on.

At the hospital, I was asked to sign some papers; then Chris was taken to x-ray. When Rick finally arrived, we were escorted to the ICU waiting room where staff rushed around preparing for their new patient. The doctor in charge needed special permission to test Chris for a possible blood clot. The test itself could cause complications, he explained, which might necessitate amputation of his leg. We gave permission to do whatever was necessary.

The test proved negative, providing relief for the moment, but then word came that Chris's blood pressure had dropped. It would be necessary to operate in order to determine his exact injuries. Again, we agreed.

After a lengthy surgery, the surgeon came to us with a burdened expression reporting multiple problems: torn liver, internal bleeding, bruised lung, and very serious head injury. We braced ourselves for the worst. His manner suggested it.

By afternoon friends and family arrived offering support as we waited. Much time was spent in the chapel, away from the noise and activity of the hospital. It was a place to quiet ourselves and pray for our son. We could weep openly there with close friends who understood the need to release endless tears. It soon became a refuge where I repeatedly prayed, "Oh, God, take care of my baby. Make him whole again."

A friend prayed, "God, Chris is special. We all love him. Yet we know You love him even more." The presence of people and the strength of many prayers pulled us through one hour and into the next, through that one and into another.

When we were finally allowed to see Chris, he had tubes in his nose, leg and throat. He was a mass of cuts and bruises, his face swollen, his body stiff and unmoving as a result of the type of brain damage he had sustained. He was in a coma. The shock of it left us standing beside his bed staring as if he were a stranger. We couldn't comprehend all that had happened in the span of a few hours. Wanting so much to gather up our family and go home, we fell prey to the inevitable question, "Why?"

The following days were filled with a series of crises. A trachcotomy was done to relieve breathing difficulties. That procedure went well, yet little hope was offered for his survival.

While we were standing in the hallway one day, the surgeon approached stating flatly, "I just don't think he is going to make it." I leaned against the wall and closed my eyes. With the pain of losing Chris so real, tears flowed unchecked. A friend accompanied us to the chapel offering what he could in the way of comfort. No one slept much that night. Too many memories slipped in like sharp little knives accentuating the painful present.

MEMORIES
As salt hurts a wound,
So do memories
Of yesterday's fleeting,
Happier hour
Sting the heart,
Accentuating
The loneliness of Now.

-Pat North

Rick felt that the doctors were treating Chris as less than a whole person - strictly as a medical problem. That exasperated him no end. He wrote at one point, "This is my son. He is more than flesh and blood. He's more than a broken body and damaged mind. Why remain silent? Why just stand there and look? He's a living soul. He's spirit."

Being limited to five minute visits per hour in the ICU, waiting got to be a way of life. Gratitude sprang up for the Women's Auxiliary which provided a variety of games, puzzles, and books for those of us stranded in hospital waiting areas. These mind-benders were a main source of relief from the frustrations of helplessness and waiting for that meager five minutes per hour.

Without our knowledge, someone notified an old friend, Rev. Jim Lawson, who lived quite a distance away. He was a black minister whose brother had been in seminary with us. Jim was a close friend of Dr. Martin Luther King, Jr., who had been slain five years before.

We again moved into the chapel, our favorite place to be alone. Jim listened carefully as we filled him in on Chris's condition. During a huddle in the little room, he urged us to become active in the healing of Chris in ways we hadn't thought of. He, too, agreed that Chris's spirit could easily be neglected while tending to his body. And he suggested that, although unconscious, Chris could still "take in" events and conversations around him.

He stressed the importance of being with Chris in a new dimension. "Talk to him. Sing to him. Let him know your loving presence is near. Have fellow ministers go in throughout the night to let Chris know someone is near."

Jim asked to see Chris, but ICU rules restricted visitors to parents and pastor. During another huddle, Rev. Jim was appointed Chris's minister and staff turned the other way as he entered the room to see his little Caucasian "parishioner." By the time Jim left he had indeed performed in the capacity of pastor. We considered him a God-send, for he had raised new possibilities for our creative involvement.

Hope sprang fresh from the desert of our despair. Jim came unannounced, but he didn't leave unnoticed, for the whole world had changed for us. We became actively engaged in the healing process of Chris within the hour.

We entered Chris's room with much zeal and determination. We could hardly wait to begin. We would no longer be passive. The helplessness we had previously experienced dissipated as we became a part of things. The stoic ICU took on an air of unusual activity as we spent our five minutes singing to Chris, telling him familiar stories, old school jokes only a boy can drag home, and laughing at our own tales. Feeling somewhat out of place with such proceedings, we paid the price of embarrassment nonetheless, in order to give Chris what little we could.

Rick wrote, "He can receive love as long as he's alive. So we will give him all we can and when we are weak, give even more. Not of our own, but of God."

So we continued to bombard his unconscious with reminders of the past and love from the present. Still, despair plagued us outside the room where the unknown took its emotional toll.

The staff continued reporting the usual consensus: "Chris is about the same. Chris is about the same. Chris is about the same." Those words were growing so wearisome. Would they ever change? Then, one ordinary day, casually tacked on those first five words, came the glorious new sound: "He's a little bit better…but don't get your hopes up."

With the admonition to quell hope from some and the more positive "He still has a chance for complete recovery" from others, we tried to keep our balance on the tightrope of conflicting prognoses from doctors who simply didn't know. It was like riding the most frightening ride at an amusement park. With each lightning quick turn of events and information, it felt as if we could be hurled into the awful space of nothingness and crash into oblivion. It was best to hold tight as reports varied from *some* hope to none.

One evening things seemed particularly futile. Chris was still unconscious. No one was offering any hope. Every day that passed without change meant less chance of Chris regaining his health. Several friends gathered in the waiting room. It was a special time. There was silence. Prayer. Weeping.

I cried softly as a friend sang the soothing words, "There is a Balm in Gilead to make the wounded whole." Then I joined him and the others in singing some of Chris's favorite songs: Jesus Loves Me, Joy to the World, Jesus Loves the Little Children. The tender caring of friends had sustained us through yet another storm.

Soon the I-V and "bink" in Chris's mouth were removed. Though still unconscious he looked much better, as if he could wake up any minute. While sitting by his bed, I noticed things I hadn't seen before: the intricate shapes of his fingers and hands. When I placed his hand in mine, it quivered, then relaxed. He'd be soft one minute, stiff the next. His body was long and bony. He had lost weight. I felt he was close to waking up. Would he? No, I knew he was far away.

On January 7th the surgeon said, "He can go to a private room. A little bit, nothing big, but we aren't expecting any big change." So few words. So much left unsaid. I decided, on the basis of his brief pronouncement, that it must not be a matter of life and death anymore. I looked at my son and thought, "Chris, come back to us. We love you." Even while the words flowed through my mind I wondered if Chris would ever be Chris again.

One morning the physical therapist met with us to give instructions on how to exercise Chris. His limbs would need someone to aid in loosening movements. The joints as well as the muscles needed to be kept "alive." In the middle of the therapist's instruction, Chris abruptly opened one eye half-way, then the other. It was the first time his eyes had opened since the accident. There was no expression, just exposed eyes. The blank stare left me with uncomfortable feelings and a lot of fear. I prayed for help with the unknown and tried to warm my chilled spirit as Chris stared beyond me into space.

Sunday, January 13th it was decided to transport Chris by ambulance to Paducah the following Tuesday. We dreaded leaving the familiarity of Jackson Hospital's friendly surroundings and staff, friends and family. It meant learning to know and trust new doctors and nurses and finding our way around a new building and routine.

Waiting for Tuesday to come, I experienced a variety of feelings: confidence that Chris would be alright, to a nagging hopelessness, plus all the in-betweens. The phrase kept coming to mind, "Lord, I believe. Help Thou my unbelief."

Rick spent the night at the hospital while I picked up Julie and went home. Julie was excited about finding her house again and immediately busied herself playing with toys. For me, it was not so easy. Everywhere I looked reminded me of Chris. Fresh tears welled up as I walked from room to room. Someone had cleaned. Everything was in order. All of Chris's toys were sitting in his room: his G.I. Joe helicopter, record player, the new things he had gotten for Christmas, and his basketball. It was too much. I thought, "Oh, Lord, I gotta make it! Chris will be home again."

With unpacking and readying Julie for bed, the grief passed. I sorted mail and wrote out some checks for the backed-up bills, then fell into a deep sleep in the comfort of my own bed for the first time in three weeks.

Western Baptist was easy enough to adjust to and by January nineteenth Chris was moved into a larger, more cheerful room. I indulged in a rising sense of optimism as I looked about. I smiled and fluffed the pillow as if to hurry things along. Just then a doctor entered the bright, new room with his somber warning that there was not a whole lot to be hopeful about. He felt that, although Chris could wake up, he could just as well stay like he was considering the severity of his head injury.

When he left, Rick and I looked into each other's eyes and silently questioned our ability to accept Chris as he was. Each detected a sad glistening in the other's eyes as the clouds of doubt gathered and the earth seemed to shudder beneath us one more time. We leaned hard on each other, sharing our mutual weakness, and asked for strength from God. Suddenly the cheerful room was nearly void of hope.

Chris had been unconscious four weeks when the doctor looked into his eyes and, with a minimum of words, said, "It's better." Accustomed by then to pushing for any scrap of information, I probed for the meaning behind his two word sentence. "Well, when he came here there was swelling. It's going down, but that might not have any effect on his condition. We'll have to wait and see." I grabbed for the bright side and encouraged myself with the meager news, "It's better."

I received word that my father would soon be released from the hospital in Selmer. Mike had already gone home. They would fully recover. A deep, deep yearning throbbed inside as I wished I could say that about Chris.

Within a few days, Chris began eating by mouth. I wrote, as I waited in Chris's room, "The sun is shining brightly. It's a beautiful day. I don't trust You, God. I will try. I just took another look outside. It's cloudy. The sun was just breaking through. I feel like that's happening in my life. You are just breaking through. I am trying to be open and receive. Don't give up on me, Lord!"

The evening of January 31st, I was sitting with Chris, watching television. Rick came. Some friends stopped by. Rick's District Superintendent visited briefly. It was quiet on the ward with a minimum of hospital bustle. We were becoming engrossed in a TV special about the life of Miss Jane Pittman when suddenly a group of five Episcopal Bishops entered the room, filling it with a certain indefinable expectancy. All had on black suits with white collars. Most of them were young men, all sincere.

After introductions (they were part of an Episcopal Convocation meeting in Paducah) a Bishop walked to the side of Chris's bed and began stroking him gently. Chris opened his eyes. A powerful silence settled on everyone gathered there. I stood at the foot of the bed overwhelmed by the tender concern shown my son by five strangers. The Bishop anointed Chris with oil. There were prayers and more silence. Gentle silence.

I felt deeply moved and comforted and, from a distance of a few feet and for the first time, I saw Chris clearly as being *God's* child. I released my frantic hold for the moment and wrote these words:

93

"Oh, Lord, as I grope for words to
capture this experience
You must know what I am feeling.
Joy. Relief. Freedom.
Chris is Your child and You love him.
I can surrender him to You, Lord,
And no matter what happens,
I know You love him
And You love me!"

Eight weeks after the accident I sat with Chris and once again looked at him closely. I thought about what a beautiful child he was with his long eyelashes and red hair...so unique. Then I startled myself with the discovery that I had forgotten the sound of his voice! It had been silent for many weeks. I looked into his eyes. They stared back. I wondered if he could hear me or see me. How I longed for a response. Even more, I desired my child to be whole again, acknowledging the persistent doubts and my own impatience. I brushed his cheek with mine, feeling his warmth, wanting so much more.

Rick, struggling to keep his spiritual head above water, wrote: "I suppose my greatest fear is that Chris will remain as he is now, with little or no improvement. I don't know that I could take this. Is it possible that God would allow this? Oh, I know it's possible. But I can't believe it or understand it. Oh, that God would grant Chris a miracle. That he could be restored to wholeness.

I do not know how prayer functions but I ask and seek and knock. Oh Lord, I pray that it's Your will that Chris may be restored to abundant life. What purpose could be served in anything less? Surely if, as some say, there is a lesson for us, then there must be a way other than through Chris's suffering and being deprived of life. I just cannot believe any such thing!

"My heart aches so. I watched Bill Walton play basketball. Red hair. Long and bony. So much like Chris. A basketball from Mom-ma, Chris's wonder a few weeks before Christmas at being able to dribble and put the ball through the hoop. He was so proud of himself.

"Oh, Chris. Oh, Lord. Oh, Spirit with power to heal. Come, Holy Spirit, come. Come and touch him. Repair the damage and bring wholeness. Breathe Thy breath upon him."

May these waters ripple once again
Beneath the sun of joy –
Lap the shore with waves of healing,
And laugh at the loss
Of Winter's icy grief,
Allowing this child to sail again
Beyond the reef of unbelief.
- Pat North

TWELVE

Inch by Inch

Four weeks after my first solo visit, my family went to see the Kirchoffs. There was noticeable improvement in Chris. He smiled and laughed appropriately at outside stimuli. Jane told how she had been working in another part of the house when she heard Chris laugh for the first time since Christmas. As he watched television, something loosened inside him and rolled out in a big guffaw. She ran in to find him thoroughly enjoying Sesame Street.

Whether Chris was responding to sight or sound wasn't important. His voice and intellect were in operation enough to comprehend a thought and give a laugh. Chris was eating better, too, and moved his head without assistance. Muscle relaxants had loosened his rigid limbs so his arms moved further on down his chest. He was generally more alert. His beautiful eyes were "alive". He blinked once for "yes", and twice for "no." Communication at last!

Julie kept asking, "Momma, when will Chrissie be well? When can Chrissie play with me?" Jane swallowed the sting inherent in her words and answered as honestly and hopefully as she could without giving any guarantees. Meanwhile, Julie brushed Chris's hair and stroked his pale skin. Sometimes she "read" him stories, or showed him pictures. When her little three year old body danced to the tune of her records, she talked to him and giggled as if hearing his answers. Maybe she could hear the unspoken better than adults who were absorbed in worry and care-giving.

Julie crawled up over the rail of the hospital bed and flopped beside Chris on her tummy. Arm stretched across his chest, she watched television and tapped his skin with her soft, pudgy fingers. Then she planted a big kiss on his cheek for no particular reason and said, "I love you, Chrissy." (Be of love a little more careful than of any other thing.)

The myriad of ways Rick and Jane had found to stimulate Chris's damaged body, mind, and spirit was impressive. They, too, stroked his skin with objects, sometimes as a game designed to call nerves and muscles back to work. They used sharp things, soft things, squishy things, warm things, cold things, wet things, dry things, rough-textured things, anything containing a message which would evoke remembrance. They reminded him of humorous incidents and laughed loudly or spoke with contrasting vocal sounds to penetrate his world.

A large mat was thrown on the floor for therapy. Rather than waste precious family time in the evenings, they put Chris on the mat and rubbed his skin or exercised his limbs while watching television or talking. Mobiles hung over Chris's bed in case he could see, for a good deal of his day was spent facing the ceiling. Colorful objects surrounded him and hanging plants adorned the eaves outside the glass door, evidence of his mother's wonderful green thumb.

Chris was carried outside and placed in a lawn chair on warm days while the family tended to gardening. Julie kept pesky bugs away so he could enjoy the fresh air and sunshine. The breeze and warmth were also part of a plan to call forth old memories. Any reminder of the past had a job to do.

Rick made up a song with words taken partly from a friend's prayer and partly from Mr. Roger's educational TV program. "You are special! You are special! You're a very special person. We love you. We love you. You're a very special person." With the soft strum of a guitar, Rick often ended the day singing to Chris as only a father can do. I thought,

> Chris knows he is loved.
> There's healing power in that.
> Chris, be loved,
> and
> Chris, be healed!"

Once the wheelchair arrived (after a frustrating wait of six months), the whole family enjoyed a new sense of freedom. Chris was then taken to movies, picnics, and church services, where his dad, being in the Good News business, talked about faith, hope, and love – drawn from a storehouse of first-hand experience.

Their unusual quality of love was probably unrecognizable to them, but to a sojourner like me, it scaled treacherous, seemingly insurmountable heights, and offered healing. Two parents found ways of loving they never knew existed, and expanded on the basic specialness which sensitized their child to God's creation. They walked in the rain, rather than avoid it. That amazed me. They thrilled together at the beauty of nature, enjoying the simplest of things, laughing often, and living at peace with the world. This was Chris's heritage.

I became keenly aware that I, with my crisis-free existence, had not learned the lessons of life as well. I had searched for meaning, looking in the shallowest places, not knowing what I wanted. I just wanted. Something was still missing. I found myself envying their sense of mission; their total physical, emotional, and spiritual commitment to their son, and the unity of their family – a unity increased through adversity.

The months wore on, pulling themselves through the knothole of time. Jane experienced recurrent cycles of hope, despair, impatience and guilt. She began to feel ingrown, concerned only with the needs of Chris, to the exclusion of other hurting people. That was not her usual way, but life didn't resemble the usual either. As the first year drew to a close and Christmas loomed large with its many painful memories, Jane wrote this prayer:

"I believe that God *is* –
Somehow, somewhere, but elusive.
Why does that have to be?
I can't seem to find the key
To unlock Your Presence to me.
I am weak. I know.
I want things the easy way.
But, Lord, my need is great.
And I keep seeking.
I'm angry! Don't play games.
I am trying. I need You most of all.
I pray for:
Healing for Chris: Can you really do that?
I don't know. Some say
You can do anything, if only asked.
Well, Lord, I've asked.
Acceptance: Lord, I want things the
way they used to be.

How close can we come?
Your Presence: I've read about it.
Heard about it.
I have a tremendous need
to *experience* Your
Presence.
LORD, HELP ME."

THIRTEEN

New Beginnings

A year after Chris's ride to the store turned into an all-out nightmare, he was taken to Children's Hospital in Memphis, Tennessee for testing and evaluation. Doctors again gave conflicting opinions as to the extent of brain damage, but one doctor presented an idea. He felt that the Institute for the Achievement of Human Potential, located in Philadelphia, Pennsylvania, should be consulted.

Rick and Jane did some checking and requested an appointment. They soon received word that Chris was scheduled for tests, evaluation, and an explanation of the program six months later. Waiting so long evoked frayed nerves and mood dips, but June finally arrived.

The initial introduction to the Institute filled them with hope. Facilities offered comfortable lounging areas and meals for entire families while patients spent five days being tested.

During their week of waiting, Rick and Jane learned about a new way of life which would entail great physical output on their parts. They must agree to give their all to the program, regardless of personal feelings. Other interests would have to wait. The prescribed therapy must be carried out to a "t." A strong vitamin regimen was prescribed for the whole family. Nutrition was discussed at length. Junk foods were off limits for Chris because of his unique physical needs. Treatment was designed to literally "feed" his brain.

Rick and Jane would also need the benefits of good, nutritious food and various vitamins to maintain their well being. Part of the vitamin regime was intended to ward off depressions. Nothing could sap the energy required to endure and apply rigors of the program. Germs must be fought off in order not to weaken Chris or cause a break in the daily program.

Rick and Jane agreed to abide by the rules set forth, except for Sunday morning church time. This was to be no half-hearted effort. They welcomed the challenge just as they had when Jim Lawson set them on a course of active participation in the chapel huddle. They were once more offered hope, but no guarantees. Hope was their lifeline.

Upon returning to Paducah, Rick commenced building the necessary equipment for therapy. Some men from his parish assisted in erecting wood beams to hold overhead pulleys. Chris would be suspended from them upside down in a special foot brace, allowing him to feed his brain oxygen and blood. An overhead ladder was needed so he could learn to walk, using his hands as "leaders." Hopefully, his legs would eventually follow suit and do their job unaided.

A springboard turtle (a suspended canvas harness) enabled Chris to dangle arms and legs at floor level in order to encourage crawling. Each piece of equipment served a unique purpose and would be used in a specified sequence of exercises. A certain number of minutes were used to apply oxygen, via a special puppet mask, between other exercises. The family room was large, allowing all necessary modifications. The stage was set, the play about to begin.

By the end of the first day on the program, Jane collapsed in a heap on the floor, moaning and groaning from exhaustion. At the same time, she snickered at her out-of-shape-ness holding her sore sides between chuckles. In spite of her lighthearted reaction to a grueling day, she wondered if and how she could repeat it again the next day. She dared not think of the days to follow for who-knew-how-long?

How in the world could she smooth out multiple mistakes she had made applying the proper sequence of oxygen? She had felt like all thumbs moving from one set of exercises to the next: so many minutes of this, so many minutes of that, oxygen, repeat this, repeat that, oxygen, etc., etc. The first week was rough going, but a flawless routine emerged in short order. They were into a new phase of adventure.

With seventy people a week still coming and going for patterning exercises during flu epidemics, the family felt an awareness of providential care as they survived the siege of sickness without incident or interruption of the program.

Physical demands of the program provided no let up. Jane eventually squeezed out funds to hire a part time helper. That enabled her to spend time with Julie, plus a little personal breathing room. She needed time to enjoy sunny fall days. With her keen admiration for nature, she had missed the freedom to bike or walk to the store. Nothing could be done without making special arrangements or packing up the wheelchair. Kicking in the leaves required preparations at home. Life had become quite complicated.

A growing dissatisfaction with her spirituality left Jane with a lot of guilt. Finding time for communion with God fell by the wayside. Days were filled with therapy and evenings tending to various neglected household duties. Free moments found her sound asleep right in the middle of reading a book or folding a pile of clothes.

Rather than losing her grip on God, it seemed to me that she was working with Him. Every move she made in therapy impressed me as a kind of devotion. I could visualize her hands moving in sync with His Hands, assisting in the healing process with each exercise. I think God must have been well pleased with her sacrifice for she had acknowledged Chris as being His child that special night in January, 1974. Anyone who takes care of God's children has His favor.

October, 1975 the Kirchoffs stopped for a visit on their way to Philadelphia for Chris's first evaluation since starting the program. There was marked improvement. He leafed through a book with his left hand, showing plenty of facial expression. Though still unable to speak, he was vocal. His right side remained immobile.

Since Saturday was a beautiful Indian Summer day, we carried Chris to the edge of a colorful wooded ravine which bordered the back of our property. The sun's warm gold bathed our woods with splendor fit for a king. While Chris lay on the blanket, a gentle breeze tousled his red hair while also rustling the leaves. It was a restful day, full of autumn's bittersweet gifts. A certain peace and longing permeated the air - so lovely, yet something was missing. That something was someone – someone we used to know.

After dinner I passed Chris, who was sitting in his wheelchair looking at a book. I chided him about getting fat. Suddenly he lurched forward, hollering like a stuck pig, and reached his left arm out as far as it would go. His face twisted with intensity as he tried desperately to communicate. I thought I had upset him with my remark but his mother, aware of her son's love for uniforms, spotted the source of his frustration and excitement.

My daughter had just returned home from a football game and was wearing an old letter jacket her boyfriend had given her. Chris wanted that jacket more than his next breath! When she took it off and put it on him, his expression turned from grimace to grin, distress to delight. Rubbing the right sleeve with his good left hand, he beamed his toothless smile all evening. When bedtime came, he held the coat on with his elbows. Jane got the message. He slept in it, but very early the next morning he left for Philly without it.

A letter came within the week saying Chris had received a good report at the Institute. They were geared up for four more months of work, work, work, armed with a new list of goals from the staff. Letters became scarce as Rick and Jane invested themselves even more fully in therapy.

February gave a sneak preview of March. Pouting, it tried to decide whether to be lion or lamb. It hadn't yet landed on which to be when Kirchoffs once more passed through our area on the way to Philadelphia. They brought their precious cargo of Julie and Chris, of course. By the time everyone had vacated the car and come through the living room door, it was obvious that Chris had changed immensely! The program had been rigorous, but a big payoff showed in no uncertain terms.

Chris's biceps resembled Popeye's. His neck girth would have been the envy of any athlete. His formerly frail body had gained weight, a good deal of which was muscle. He had good control of head movements and could feed himself with his left hand. Legs that had been so tightly drawn up when I first visited him were now able to take exaggerated baby steps, flailing the air, while someone held him. He laughed when people made faces, a game he loved, so my husband tried out some dandies for Chris's entertainment.

Right in the middle of a grotesque contortion, Chris reached out and grabbed Dick's tongue, giving it a good, firm twist. Chris howled with laughter as we all rolled on the floor amid waves of glee. We celebrated Chris's intact sense of humor and physical victories, knowing he had come so far. I impulsively took a poster from the wall, rolled it up, and put it in their suitcase to take home. It said, "Patience is not passive. It is active. It is concentrated strength." They knew all about patience.

As soon as everything settled down, we brought out two boxes. One contained a gift for Julie. The other was for Chris. It was the old blue letter jacket that had captured his affection months before. Embossed on the back of it were new letters: CHRIS KIRCHOFF. He displayed the same excitement for the threadbare thing, and again wore it all evening, along with his infectious smile. Then he wore it to bed, where I suppose his dreams played out scenes of him crossing the goal line.

The next day was dark and windy, cold and wet   a lion kind of day. Nonetheless, Rick invited everyone to go for an ice cream treat.

Chris sat huddled up in the front seat with his letter jacket on. The rest of us squeezed in the back two seats of their station wagon.

As we headed down the highway, mischievous giggles from the far back seat caught our attention. We turned to see our young passengers holding up Chris's extra large reading therapy flash cards for the driver behind us. The gentleman followed long enough to read such proclamations as "Pepper is our cat…Cat kisses are yucky…They hang me upside down." The man passed by with a curious smile on his face.

HEY, NUMBER FORTY-FOUR!

None of us knew,
When you were three years old
And wearing jersey number forty-four
Drooping past your underwear,
That you'd be playing
In a game of Life and Death
A few years hence.
Of course not!
But then,
Neither did we know that you,
Chris Kirchoff,
Had it in you
To sink the ball
Or score a touchdown
Or hit a homer
In the big, big game of Life
At age seven.
Y'know what?
BIG guys have hit homers
Yet never "won" –
Sunk the ball
Yet never scored
Like YOU have!
For you have moved the heart of God
And squashed defeat beneath your heel
By training like a "pro."
Let's hear it for number fo'ty fo'!

FOURTEEN

One in a Thousand

When our friends left for the northeast the next morning, I began counting down for my own upcoming weekend adventure. A retreat workshop billed "Healing and Wholeness", led by Rev. Evelyn Carter, was scheduled just a mile away. Though skeptical, events of the past couple of years had peaked my interest. I thought, "This could be my answer." It was worth investigating. Since my husband had a special invitation to attend and evaluate the workshop as a professor and pastor, I could tag along.

My personal agenda, of course, centered on Chris. Still raging inside about the lack of understanding what suffering was all about, and Chris's limited recovery, I hoped for an opportunity to talk it out with Rev. Ev, as she was affectionately called. So why was I so uneasy about stepping into strange territory? As the weekend approached, I tensed up.

Friday evening we filed up the steps of a historic little white country church with many other people. As we entered the foyer, my eyes met with those of Rev. Ev. I guess I expected some kind of formal introduction, but she greeted us with the softest, warmest, biggest smile I'd ever seen on a human being. Rev. Ev. had a striking manner. She was a large woman, matched by her sweeping personality. Her dark brown eyes and face shone with the love of God as if lit by heavenly light bulbs!

As Rev. Ev got into the service and shared her heart, I found myself regretting the absence of Kirchoffs. If only they could have joined us. If only

After a time of singing and greeting one another, we broke into small groups to discuss her opening comments. I was assigned to

Rev. Ev's group, along with my husband and several pastors. In spite of the warm initial meeting with her, I felt on edge. "On edge" might be more accurately described as "transparent." Impatience was part of the mix, too.

The clergy fired typical intellectual questions at her, leaving me on the outside looking in. I had a million questions, but feared verbalizing even my main one: "What about Chris?" Taking the role of spectator, I removed myself from the circle on the floor and took a front row seat. Rev. Ev saw that as meaning more than physical discomfort. She sensed that I had "left" the group, resisting any active participation. She was right. I closed up for the duration.

There was no doubt that Rev. Ev was exclusively God's. Her spirit was refreshing; unlike anyone else I had met. Her sense of humor had a disarming and delightful quality, but a distance quickly formed between us. An unspoken "something" created a gulf – and deep disappointment. She had not reached out to me as I'd hoped. But then, that was one of my weak points in earlier years – always expecting someone to come to me. She wasn't about to do the coming. Because of that, my anxiety and anger intensified.

The next day, Rev. Ev fielded a question and answer time, which soon snowballed into personal interchanges with many. In her unique style, she began working with people one-on-one in a low-key conversational format. Soon participants experienced relief from all sorts of difficulties. I was excited to see first hand what I had only read and heard about. At the same time, a gnawing dis-ease was growing. I wished she would reach out to me as she was the others.

I took a little mental journey into the past two years while the workshop continued. What a terrible blow the Kirchoffs had suffered, and how helpless I'd felt. I wasn't even close to understanding why it happened. What was the point? Memories poured in of various pastors and retreats and Bible studies where I had tried so hard to find answers.

I was so wrapped up in Chris I couldn't think of much else. Why was he so important? Most people felt badly for the family's tragedy and did what they could, but that wasn't the nature of my involvement. I was all-consumed with it. A crucial issue was at stake. I didn't even know what the issue was. I just knew it had to do with me and God. God wasn't delivering any answers. He wasn't dealing out much comfort either. I grew more uneasy with every passing day. Here I was at a healing seminar, where it could be discussed openly, and I couldn't open my mouth.

I had been brusque with a lot of Christians through the years. Too often their cut and dried theories on the meaning of suffering failed to make a dent. Oh, for someone who knew the meaning. Someone who would show it to me. Rev. Ev knew plenty, but she was busy.

I had retreated into myself as the meeting progressed. Rev. Ev signaled to a girl who was sitting beside and in front of me, asking if she would like to talk, but I thought her gaze and comments were directed to me. A grin befitting a little kid who had become the focus of attention spread across my face. Finally - the agony of this mysterious journey through suffering would be relieved. I had Rev. Ev's full attention!

It took a moment to realize that Rev. Ev's focus wasn't set on me at all. Embarrassed to realize she was addressing herself to someone else, I struggled to regain my inner composure. My self talk took on a pouty tone: She's helping everyone else, why can't she do the same for me? If the Holy Spirit can reveal such detailed knowledge to her concerning others, couldn't and shouldn't He do that for me? Doesn't He know how much I need help understanding this mess?

PRAYER

Oh, God.
Oh, Father.
Where are You when I'm alone?
If You're so great to be around,
To have nearby,
Why aren't You?
Do I have to be near death
Before You come to me?
Don't You know I need You
When I'm just un-crisised me?
Just me?
Do I have to scare it out of You?
Are You my Father?
Surely, if You are,
You'll come to me
Just for the fun of it!

By evening I had worked up nerve to approach her. There wasn't much time left. She would leave after the morning service, so I swallowed my pride and took a seat across from her at the dinner table. With a good deal of apprehension, I opened the conversation with details about Chris, noting that no one else had mentioned healing for others, only themselves. That seemed safe, and commendable on my part. She seemed unimpressed with my prideful observation, in fact distant, as she gnawed on a drumstick. That angered me.

Feeling on shaky ground, I persevered with Chris's story and my frustration with God. Her reply was blunt, bordering on flip, as she asked me point blank: "Do you trust God with Chris?" She managed to bore a hole right through me while looking past my startled expression into space.

Trust God with Chris? She had to be kidding. I didn't trust God with anything at that point. Why, I didn't even *know* Him. She knew. I answered rather limply, with a tinge of martyrdom, "I don't know." She would certainly have to admire my honesty, if nothing else. But my honesty landed like a boomerang right around my spiritual neck.

She said, "Well, then, if you don't know, why bother talking about it?" With a roll of her big brown eyes, and a wave of her big brown hand, I had been dismissed. That was the last straw. The church had nothing to offer, nor did she.

I stormed out of the room, leaving my husband to find his own way home. He was having the time of his life, but as often happened, I found myself at odds with all things religious. Like a teenager leaving home after a family feud, I spun gravel and vowed never to return. I mentally chewed the lady to shreds on the way home, extending my rage to all church people everywhere. I'd have no more of it!

The tantrum followed me into the house, gaining momentum as I fantasized how guilt-ridden she would be if I died as a result of her insensitivity. Maybe then she'd think twice before treating someone else's feelings so coldly. Couldn't she see that I was genuinely searching for answers? A listening ear? Oh, I might as well tip up a bottle of pills and forget it.

The downward spiral was a repeat of my emotional tantrum in Dr. B.'s office, which landed me in Wolverine country with two kids and ten bucks! Someone would have to come and get me and take me home where it was safe and calm. But I was alone. No one was there but me. And no one would be coming.

Instead of swallowing pills, I went to bed, sobbing with embarrassment and self pity. My nose ran a mile a minute as I buried myself under the covers and gasped for air. Tears and chokes persisted as I began to sweat, in more ways than one.

Having gone to bed to withdraw and pout, I did a pretty good job of it for awhile. But within minutes, a strange thing happened. Someone did come to get me and take me home. Mysteriously, my feelings shifted. With the arrival of the Holy Spirit, I suddenly sat up and wailed like a lost child. Belligerent tears gave way to repentant tears. Fury turned into confession, hardness into softness.

I vocalized every ugliness I owned – like bubbles rising in a bottle of liquid. Each one represented a sin. As each rose to the surface of my awareness, it burst on contact when reaching the Light of God. Each bubble had a name, each name was a game: manipulation, rebellion, pride, unbelief, etc. I had finally gotten up close and personal with God, my Father. As I claimed responsibility for all my unpleasantries, large and small, He accepted me as if there were none. Each time I admitted a game, I let go of it, realizing the price had already been paid for all such things.

Free of concern about my imperfections, I felt newly worthwhile. Relaxing the fight within that had made me such a nuisance to myself and others, I sensed loving Arms closing around me. I declared right out loud, "God, I feel like giving You a great big hug!" In that moment, He hugged *me* into new life – abundant life; a fulfillment of the love demonstrated the day Dr. B. held me in the hallway and let me cry.

Rev. Ev was right not to have bitten the "Poor Chris, poor me" bait. Chris was not the real issue in my life. My anger with God was the issue. My unbelief. The lack of honest relationship with Him. I had been chasing a phantom for years, using Chris's tragedy as a weapon against belief that God is God. Period. He couldn't be conned. What I needed most was to look inside. I had trod this way before in a therapist's office. It was time to move on.

I hadn't counted on Rev. Ev's intimate relationship and obedience to her Heavenly Father to be the stopping point for my running battle with Him. I ran into that wall head-on, not knowing what hit me until I looked back from a distance of forgiveness. She had such close communication with Him that her response to me was in exact proportion to my need. I have never been the same since her crucial question: "Do you trust God with Chris?"

FATHERLY ADVICE

Patricia, dear,
You've camped at the foot of this mountain
Long enough!
It's time to move on over
To the other side.
Follow Me
And see what treasures
I have waiting there for you.

FIFTEEN

The Spirit in '76

A barrel of trouble rolled in on the heels of the life-changing weekend with Rev. Ev, testing our newfound joy to the max. The cat bit our neighbor, causing permanent damage to a tendon, and putting us on edge while waiting to see if the cat was rabid. Our cars broke down every other day, making transportation to jobs located in opposite directions a nightmare.

Our oldest son's wife left him after just six months of marriage, and our younger son was caught in some distressing behavior. It was all beyond our ability to control. Calls to Rev. Ev provided limited comfort. Her advice was to "stand fast." Eventually, plans were made for a move to north-central Ohio, where Dick would pastor three rural churches. Only our two younger children would go with us.

I prayed for an angel for the son who wasn't yet grounded in faith. A few months later, a stranger stopped him on a busy city street and put in motion a chain of miraculous events. By early fall, our entire family had come together in a new dimension of love and faith. God had indeed sent an angel, and was about to give me an unexpected blessing.

Nineteen hundred and seventy-six was a big year for America, with lots of fireworks and special events marking the nation's bi-centennial birthday. It was also a big year for me. I had begun a journey that wouldn't stop. Being in earnest about knowing Kingdom things for myself, I stepped into new situations out of curiosity, as well as for something more satisfying spiritually.

We had moved to a country parish, causing a dramatic change in lifestyle. Our tiny community offered a considerably slower pace and more tranquil atmosphere. I took advantage of the lazy summer and began writing this book. By the end of August I felt stymied as to what should be done with it. Chris had reached a plateau. Rick and Jane were discouraged. Nothing seemed to be moving. My "happy ending" was missing.

Something deep down felt odd. Intense. Prayerful. I felt increasingly moved to pray for Chris, probably best described in my former church history as being "burdened." Just as I had prayed for an angel for my son, I prayed for Chris. A curious sense of being "positioned" gripped me. I recognized the Hand of God and did my best to follow His lead all week long.

During that time I ventured into a nearby town to attend a Christian businessmen's meeting. Women guests were included. I sat across the table from a humble farm couple who spoke freely of their prayers for sick people, and the miraculous recoveries they had witnessed. Chris came to mind, and I felt a rise of expectation and faith as I listened. Impulsively, I asked the president of the group for permission to speak briefly.

It was uncharacteristic for me to speak in front of anyone, especially strangers. The words came easy as I told Chris's story, my struggle, the desire to see him well, and how I was waiting for the Lord to write the last chapter of his story. People gathered and prayed for Chris as I stood in proxy for him.

I had scarcely gotten into my house before second-guessing myself. What in the world had I done? Were those people crazy? Was I? I had cautions about the happy, confident bunch, but could hardly contain my unexplainable excitement. There was no denying my inner buoyancy.

My family dispersed as soon as the meeting had ended. Dick made some parish calls while my daughter and youngest son went shopping. With a newly licensed driver at the wheel, I threw God a "quickie": "You'll have to take care of them, Lord. I don't have time to worry about it."

Alone at last, that firm, gentle nudging returned. I had the strongest desire to call Jane. Should I? What would I say? She would know I wasn't calling to pass the time of day. Would I dare risk telling her about the strange events taking place in my neck of the woods? She had been hurt too many times by well-meaning, but often insensitive, Christians. Some had offered across-the-board miracles for Chris, only to disappear once they didn't materialize. Others had blamed Chris's lack of recovery on their lack of faith. I didn't want to add insult to injury, but I did want to share my experiences of the week.

Resisting apprehensions, I dialed the numbers that connected me with Jane's familiar southern drawl. "Hay-lo", followed by her more personal "Way'll, h'ah, Pay-it." She always sounded like she had just dripped out of a honeycomb.

I asked, as casually as I could, how Chris was. Just as casually, she replied that she was just about to write and tell me the news. Chris had spoken his first word since the accident earlier that week! I caught my breath as she proceeded. "Just a minute. I'll let you hear for yourself." Before I had time to absorb what she had said, I heard it. Chris, with deliberate effort and discernable pride, spoke the most precious "Mom-ma" imaginable. It left me speechless.

I just began to cry, and tried to swallow the great swell of happiness rising in my throat. After three years of silence, Jane had finally heard her son's forgotten voice. We talked for a few minutes while I explained a little of what had happened before I called, then hung up in a bucket of tears.

Frantic to tell someone, I ran to the neighbor's house. Afraid I'd explode before getting there, I quickened the pace. She was always home. Not this time. How unusual.

I ran back home and did a curious thing; I dropped an old Christmas record on the turntable and cranked it up to top volume. It played over and over for an hour and a half, its words breaking over my spirit with the thundering crash of ocean breakers. "Joy to the world, the Lord is come!" Every carol was like a cloudburst of glory. The music was alive, and so was I. It was as if Christ had been born in the stable of my heart all over again, and His Spirit had come to reside there for good.

I was deeply, serenely happy. Chris had spoken. By the end of an hour and a half of profuse tears, and what I would describe as pure worship of the Most High God, my eyes felt bruised with tears. The residue of unbelief and doubt washed away with each revolution of the record.

I thanked God that Chris could speak, if only one word. Even more, I felt an enormous relief inside, for I had once more experienced the mighty, tender presence of God's Holy Spirit. It was much different than our first meeting. I was overflowing with worship, thanksgiving, praise, and joy – and *a need to tell it*.

When my family returned home, I hardly knew where to begin. They were thrilled with the news of Chris, but I couldn't scratch the surface of my intimate hour and a half with God. My husband asked if I would like to share the news with our three congregations the next morning. I wasn't sure about making another public appearance so soon after what felt like a melodramatic presentation at the businessmen's meeting. Recalling my blubbering failure to recite a Christmas verse when I was five gave me pause, too. I said I would see in the morning.

The congregation was quite sparse because of Labor Day weekend. A lot of folks were away. Funny, but I was disappointed – an unusual response for someone who dreaded crowds and usually stayed in the background. Without notice, a group of fifty people from a local camping club filed in and filled the empty seats. I signaled Dick that I would tell my story. He called me forward early in the service. I stepped out with a brand new boldness to speak of Jesus Christ. The more people, the better!

With newborn confidence, my words flowed just as I had hoped they would. Feeling deeply satisfied, I closed my talk with a statement: "The day Chris is healed these church chimes are going to play Christmas carols, even if it's the middle of July!" Halfway down the aisle, applause erupted. I looked up to see tears in many eyes, including those of our visitors. God had won some new cheerleaders for Chris, as well as Himself.

I rode the three-point church circuit that morning, sharing twice more. We sang the carol "Joy to the World" in a little white frame country church surrounded by fields of corn, soybeans, and cows. Maybe it was my imagination, but I thought the cows rolled their eyes that warm morning when we sang carols out of season. I prayed that one day those villages would hear chimes ringing carols in July. Why? So the question "What's going on?" could be answered by people who knew that the glory of the Lord had been freshly revealed. Oh, what a day that would be!

SIXTEEN

Discovery, Confession, Surrender

A few months after the cows rolled their eyes, my newly-converted son gave me a Bible for Christmas. I immediately began a cover-to-cover exploration of Scripture. God said I'd find the meaning of the dancing seal there. Plodding through parts of the Old Testament, I made my way through its pages with a voracious appetite for God's Word. Consuming chapters and whole books in one reading became commonplace. The reading race accelerated once I reached the pages of Job.

Once my eyes fell on its pages, something out of the ordinary happened. It was as if the words had fish hooks on the ends of them. I couldn't get away; didn't want to! Coming across a portion of Scripture which had been used in a sermon I had heard weeks earlier, I got hooked all the way through to the core of my being. It so clearly described what had been my experience. Job was not a dead historical account of a man's life; it was an up-to-date account of mine. My name might as well have been on the printed page.

God, over the course of many years, had spoken to me in each of these ways. Reading Job, I recalled the countless times that God had spoken to me through dreams, through the sickness of others - mainly Chris - through a messenger, Evelyn Carter, "one in a thousand who will show a man [and me] what is right." The grace of God broke through as I read on.

Job had indulged himself in a lot of questions during his period of suffering. He eventually fell prey to pride, defending himself through it all. Had I not done that, too? I had defended my good intentions as being noble and worthy of Rev. Ev's attention, not to mention God's responsibility to give me answers. It had seemed forever since God had spoken to me before the night Ev and I locked horns. He was similarly "absent" during Job's prolonged crying out.

Job had a fellow linger nearby called Elihu who patiently talked about the nature of God and His creation. Elihu made all the difference because he brought things into focus for Job. Rev. Ev did the same beautiful thing for me with a brief question: "Do you trust God with Chris?" Her question changed the course of my life. It set my feet a'dancing to a different spiritual tune…the beat of faith.

My spirit was wholly caught up in Elihu's exquisite exhortation. Something sprang to life as I read about the majesty of God, which not only captured my imagination – but set it loose.

In Chapter 37 Elihu says, "…Job, stand still and consider the wondrous works of God." I, too, stood still and considered His wondrous works as, in Chapter 38, God Himself speaks. He not only speaks, He unfolds a most beautiful flow of poetic wisdom, going on and on about His matchless creation. He delights in discussing and describing things of nature, particularly the animal life He designed and brought forth.

In a rare moment, He talks about His own wisdom in terms of the distinct differences He designated in the animal kingdom; how he made them, why He equipped them in certain ways. He began the discourse with a question, and followed it with 85 more! But His questions *were* answers. That's how God chose to deal with Job and me – out of the whirlwind of His own words.

Chapter 41 contains great detail about the crocodile. Who would think God could be so fascinated with a crocodile? I caught my breath and spilled some tears as I read the words of God. He finished by talking about how Job, like all other men, was fearful of the crocodile above all other beasts. And, as is common to man, he doesn't know enough to fear the beast's Creator! My former rebellion and I-can-handle-things-better-than-You-can attitude were dangerously close to my remembrance. That lured me into yet more powerful scripture in Chapter 42:3-6, where I acknowledged my error and made my confession, along with Job:

"Therefore I now see I have rashly uttered what I did not understand, things too wonderful for me, which I did not know…I had heard of You (only) by the hearing of the ear; but now my spiritual eye sees You. Therefore, I loathe my words and abhor myself, and repent in dust and ashes."

In my heap of "dust and ashes", I surrendered. Something that had been flopping around, wanting to die, finally did. And something that yearned to be born was born. God's Spirit-breathed Book did that for me, while granting an entrance of peace; the exquisite gift which only comes through belief that *He is*. He reigns. He can be trusted with all things. He cares enough to talk to man (and woman) in such a simple, profound way. He loved me enough to melt me with His Word.

DESIRE

Oh, the rootage sinks yet deeper
As the glory of God waters this earth (me)
And I more firmly grasp
The soil that has been there all along –
His everlastingness,
Faithfulness,
Perfection,
Justice,
Promise.
I feel a deepening,
A reaching into bedrock,
A finality of Faith-quest,
A beginning of Faith-land.
Yet, take me deeper, Lord God.
Cause me to hunger and thirst
Far more than I know now.
Saturate me with Holy Spirit life,
And teach me Truth
From all You have created.

SEVENTEEN

EPILOGUE

About the same time I had come to rest regarding Chris's safety in God's hands (1976), Jane had a remarkable dream which also brought her troubled spirit to rest. The dream went unshared (with me) until recently. It might never have come to my attention if it hadn't been for earthly circumstances and Heaven's mysterious ways.

In one of my occasional letters to Jane, I mentioned some health problems my daughter was having. Jane, being a nurse, perked up her professional ears and called to inquire about the gal who used to play "tent" with her son.

By the time Jane called, Shellie's symptoms had disappeared and tests had proved negative. Jane isn't prone to write letters, so she turned the conversation into a "catch-up" time. "How's Dick? How's the new church coming along? What keeps you busy these days?"

After listening carefully to life in my little corner of the world, she asked if I'd like to get a peek at theirs. She said Rick had been featured on a television series titled, "Imagine A World Without Easter." She offered to send a DVD so we could see it. I said, "Sure! We'd love to see it." It arrived a few days later, but I laid it aside for later viewing; later being when we got back from vacation, which was at the door.

Upon our return home, Shellie and her husband stopped in for a visit. I asked if they would like to watch it with us, since we hadn't seen it yet. Shellie jumped at the chance to see our former neighbors for the first time in decades. We all settled back for an evening with Rick and his congregation.

The service began with traditional Easter music and a panoramic view of choir and church-goers. What a beautiful church Rick pastored! Soon our tall, lanky friend stepped to the pulpit, minus most of his hair. He had gone the way of many another preacher…bald. A group chuckle broke our concentration for an instant, but Rick's still soft, warm-with-Tennessee drawl grasped our full attention. He had turned out to be an impressive, articulate preacher.

Rick was nearing the end of his sermon when he introduced the story of a man whose wife had died at a fairly young age. As if caught in a riptide of grief too overpowering to fight, the young husband despaired of life. An intense season of inner darkness shredded his emotions in the months to follow. But the man eventually broke through, attributing his ability to step into a good future to the discovery of God's resurrection power. Because that power had carried him safely through personal crisis, he knew it could get him through anything to come.

Rick's voice rose with excitement as he agreed with the man's statement. I sensed the approach of something unusual – something about Chris. Leaning forward, I strained to catch every word. Rick piggy-backed the man's proclamation with animated affirmation:

"And it will! It will! I understand that in a deeply personal way. My son Chris was severely injured in an automobile accident when he was six years old. Though he survived, he would never be the same. In that accident Chris was brain injured, profoundly and permanently disabled, able to speak only a word or two, confined to a wheelchair. He would require lifetime, around-the-clock care. Living with that reality left me with questions -questions about God's promise for someone like Chris.

A gracious answer to my questions came in a dream my wife shared with me on Father's Day, about three years after the accident. (WHAT? I wasn't aware of any such dream!) In it, Jane was pushing Chris in a wheelchair uphill in a lush forest. It was late summer. Leaves had begun to fall and cover the ground. Fall colors were everywhere.

A path wound up the hill, and Jane was struggling to push Chris's wheelchair along the steep path. Finally, she made it to the top, and saw a beautiful valley below. In that valley was a beautiful lake. Jane eased Chris downhill, and down into the lake. The water was warm and clean. Chris motioned that he wanted to get into the water, so Jane slipped him out of his chair. He was floating on water, loving the feel and freedom of it. Now on this lake, in the center, there was a bright mist. The mist made a dividing line between one side of the lake and the other side.

Jane could see Chris, but could not go up to him. And on this other side, something wonderful happened. Chris got up out of the water. He stood. His body straightened, and he began to walk around. He moved freely and gracefully. Then he spoke. He spoke with ease and clarity. Jane was amazed and excited and incredibly happy. As she watched Chris, it began to grow dark - dark everywhere - except in the mist. Jane called to Chris, "Chris, it's getting dark. It's time to go home! Come on, Chris, it's getting darker. It's time to go home!"

But he simply smiled from the mist and said, "No, Mom! Look at me! I AM home! I don't want to go back. I AM home!" When Jane awoke, she awoke with a reassurance that this dream was a gift of God, a hope-filled gift, reminding her and me that, for all of us, Chris's promise is that when we cross that great misty Divide, through the love of Christ, we can be home and be whole. And in that belief, we are given the gift of courage for today and hope for tomorrow."

I gulped in a gush of air as the DVD wound to an end, astounded that I had just heard about Jane's dream for the first time. This manuscript had lain on a shelf for over 30 years, gathering dust in wait of a fitting conclusion. The conclusion had been locked up in Jane's unshared dream all that time, but suddenly it had been set free. What a treasure Jane had sent. And what an extraordinary Father's Day gift Rick had received.

God's gift would reach beyond two hurting parents, freshly encouraged in the still of night, to countless other persons who are caught in similar circumstances. Those whose hearts have also been wounded with tragedy, draped with a heavy cloak of sorrow, and fogged in with questions minus answers, would get a lifeline of hope from Jane's dream.

Before retiring for the night, I determined to appropriate God's resurrection power regarding this story, which has awaited its ending for several decades. His grace in the lives of a formerly suicide-prone woman, whose life intersected with that of a little boy and his loving family, must be told. Each of us had somehow emerged from years of faith-fog, which is no small thing. I pulled out the long-neglected manuscript the following morning to experience revival of a dream that had been all but laid to rest.

By the end of the week, I had organized my thoughts, re-read the manuscript, and turned over some cover ideas in my mind. Having already decided on the title, I visualized something depicting fog.

We spent Sunday afternoon mingling with our congregation down by the riverside – the Ohio River-side. Our hosts, Kevin and Pam, had opened their summer camp property for a hog roast, so I spent some lazy hours watching the shimmering water. A conversation behind me caught my attention. Kevin mentioned how foggy it had been during waning summer days. Fog! Aha! My mind's wheels turned at breakneck speed, well oiled by Jane's dream.

I broke my lazy daze and hurried to the deck, where Pam was enjoying the summer sunshine. I told her about my old, yellowing manuscript, Jane's dream, and my desire to finish the story. I also asked permission to come onto her property some foggy morning to photograph. Though no one would be there weekdays, she told me to help myself.

A peek out the bedroom window early the following morning sealed my day's agenda. It was a wonderful fog-choked pre-dawn! I hurriedly dressed, grabbed camera and keys and stepped into a perfect pea-soup morning for my solo adventure down by the riverside.

I hadn't yet reached the end of my street when I detected a thumping. It took a moment to realize that it was just my excited little heart! The anticipation and worry that the sun would rise before I could get to Pam's property had thrown it into high gear. I pressed the gas pedal slowly, being extra cautious in what I considered to be a divinely ordained fog cover. Several miles and moments later, I pulled my dew-sprinkled van onto Pam's lot, facing the riverbank.

Fog had suddenly taken on a whole new dimension of mystery, magnifying my ignorance of its unique personality. It had previously been something to look at, not something to be in. But that day would be different; I had turned into a granny and Chris had turned into a man. And we had each come out of life's confusing fog in spite of the odds.

I felt strange driving onto Pam's property in the dark. Neighbors weren't even up yet, but they had undoubtedly heard the crunch of gravel and a groaning engine coming to a halt. What if they thought I was an intruder and called the police? Would my explanation of wanting to photograph rising mist pass muster? The river wasn't visible at 6:30 a.m. It was "socked in" big time. That was a *good* thing.

Exiting the van with camera in hand, I strolled to the riverbank for a closer study of the surroundings. Overlooking the river was a steep bank, lined with trees on one side, and a clear view of the meandering Ohio River (when fog lifted) to the west. An excellent simulation of Jane's dream scene should emerge with the rising sun, whenever it chose to appear.

Not yet understanding the way of fog, I poised the camera for action, thinking the event was imminent. At least I had made it in time, despite driving slowly. In minutes, I relaxed my grip. There was no sign of imminent light. And morning mist was wet! The lens sported speckles of sprinkles, while my clothes took on a surprising amount of moisture. Learning that mist does not make for a good hair day, I walked back to the protection of a dry van to await the "event."

An hour passed with no event. Darkness clung like a wet blanket. Having felt fairly shouted out of bed to capture the miracle of sunlight piercing and lifting morning mist left me feeling a bit foolish. I glanced to the east, straining to see the slightest hint of light. No deal. A sigh of impatience, and turn of the door handle, and I once more strolled the property to the edge of an invisible river. Growling river barges churned by, moving me into a game of "Which way did it go?"

Somehow, discerning their course (either downriver or upriver) took some of the sting out of having no fog savvy. Again getting dampened down with mist, I climbed into the van to wait it out. Cracking the window kept wetness out, allowing bird chirps and the sound of laboring barge engines in. It wasn't so bad listening to God's world in solitude, but two hours of waiting tested my limits.

The third hour was running out when the temptation to leave and come back another day almost overtook me. I had never seen a day that didn't eventually dawn, so I stuck it out. Suddenly something in the atmosphere changed. The huge spider web on the deck rail began swinging to and fro, and the sky lightened, as if getting serious about clearing things up. The woods came alive with activities of birds and leaves, both of which glided to the wet grass on a fresh breath of air. The "event" was about to happen!

Nervous about how quickly sunlight might dissipate fog, I hustled to the riverbank with camera aimed straight ahead. The magic moment sluggishly lingered behind the stubborn gray wall of mist, so I moved further down the property line, keeping a wary eye for quick changes. Before another bird chirped, my waning patience was rewarded with breaking dawn. On the heels of my rising excitement came a rising sun.

At first glance, it seemed as if my eyes were playing tricks on me. Detecting the faintest suggestion of landscape on the opposite shore, I blinked to clear my eyes. Was something there? Another blink allowed just enough time for things to clarify. As if "poofed away" by someone, fog dissipated. What had been there all along, completely hidden from human view, was revealed; homes, barns, trees, river barges, sky, and the river itself. Huge coal barges I had only noticed by sound for three hours now plied sun-splashed waters.

Racing back and forth, I photographed from every angle until satisfied that I had completed my mission, then took a long look at the spectacular miracle of early dawn and turned to leave.

Rounding the bend of a dirt lane gave me one more opportunity to view the snaking Ohio River. Pausing to savor the moment, I faced my inability to capture God on film. Rather, I faced God's ability to capture *me* in the process of trying.

During my hours of solitude down by the riverside, a still-developing theology deepened. The river did it. It taught me a lot about life. Life is like a river. It has its steady, predictable currents and flow, as well as raging, overwhelming torrents, brought on by harsh storms. When smaller streams get too full and overflow their banks, chaos follows. Rushing to the river, out of control rivulets pick up and carry every imaginable bit of refuse and debris, emptying it into the jaws of a mightier flow. Unwanted debris, such as submerged dead logs wash into the river, making water pleasures impossible for a season. Such is life.

The river greets dark dawns strangled with heavy, bone-chilling mist. It also welcomes sunny, carefree days. It offers enjoyment for some, but tragedy for those who get caught in its dangerous undertow. The river rises and falls according to prevailing conditions; conditions it can't control. Human emotions rise and fall with varying circumstances that are beyond their control, too.

The river separates one shore from another. Life does that, suspending us between earth and heaven by just a breath. There's a whole faith-world to be discovered down by the riverside.

The river lay to my left as I pulled away. Funny, but when I turned the corner and glanced in my rear-view mirror, I thought I saw a Dancing Seal frolicking between the shores; not the shores of Ohio and Kentucky, but the shores of Here and There – the shores of Time and Eternity. He looked like a carbon copy of Someone I had encountered so often on my tempestuous journey – the Person of the Holy Spirit – God's creative, skillful Spirit who is able to accomplish extraordinary feats in very ordinary lives. Yes, I'm *sure* I saw the Dancing Seal!

SONSHINE

Sonshine –
Warming through,
Reaching the undergrowth
Of hurt and shame
To make it better;
Healing broken bones
Of self-esteem.
The Son is bright enough
To bore through every
Fog-choked moment.
He's warm enough
To heal each break
And soothe each ache.
He's full of grace and glory!

-by the author
Copyright 1985
"I'll Chase The Spring"

Postscripts

From Rick and Jane:

  In the early days of Chris's injury a minister friend came to us and said, "Rick, Jane, I want you to know that if you don't get a healing, you'll get a resurrection." At the time, our reaction to this affirmation was pretty much like Pat's reaction to her friend, Rev. Ev.

  Yet, years later, we look back on those words about healing and resurrection and celebrate their simple, profound truth. No, we didn't get a healing – at least in the way we wanted, or when we wanted it. But we got the promise of the resurrection. And today that seems quite enough.

  Somewhere along the way, perhaps most clearly after the dream, we were both able to put aside questions, doubts, and anger. We were able to simply trust God with Chris. We were able to trust Chris into those two strong Hands that Rick first saw as he drove behind the ambulance.

  There are still profound challenges. And there are days when we are caught in the grip of grief – mostly now on anniversaries or at times when other people's kids achieve something big, or arrive at some milestone. But most days are filled with joy, meaning, and laughter. And Chris is a big part of that laughter. His smile is contagious. His sense of humor is constant. His positive outlook is unflappable. He is a gift – just as he is.

Chris, 2005

About the Kirchoffs

The Kirchoff family resides in Germantown, Tennessee, where Rick pastors the Germantown United Methodist Church. Jane entered the nursing profession shortly after Chris's accident, and works as an R.N. in a local hospital's Same Day Surgery Unit. Julie is a beautician, and lives in the Germantown area. Chris continues to delight his family, friends, and caretakers with his intact sense of humor. The ongoing inspiration of his life is a source of strength and joy to all who know his story. Chris turned 39 years old Valentine's Day, 2006.

Rev. Rick and Jane Kirchoff

About the Norths

Author Patricia North and her pastor husband, Dick, celebrated their 50th wedding anniversary June 4, 2005. They have been pastoring churches for 40 years, the last 16 being at Christ United Methodist Church, located in Portsmouth, Ohio. Their ministry there is a reflection of their triumph and the fulfillment of their dreams for…

To be fulfilled has a spiritual root,
And the root is what feeds the tree.

Rev. Dick and Pat North

To Order Copies of

Out of the Mist

by **Patricia North**

I.S.B.N. 1-59879-103-6

Order Online at:
www.authorstobelievein.com